There's Been A Change Of Plans

A Memoir about Divorce, Dating and Delinquents in Mid-Life

The author has tried to recreate events, locales and conversations from her memories of them. In order to maintain their anonymity in some instances she has changed the names of individuals and places and she also may have changed some identifying characteristics and details such as physical properties, occupations and places of residence.

Published by Martin Brown Publishers, LLC
1138 South Webster Street
Kokomo, Indiana 46902
www.mbpubs.com

ISBN 13: 978-1-937070-62-5

Amy Koko

is a contributor to Huffington Post Divorce, Over 50 and Women sections. She has written for First Wives Social Network and Creative Loafing, a local publication. She has been an active blogger, exwifenewlife.com , since 2011.

You can follow Amy

on Twitter at https://twitter.com/female50freaked or friend her on Facebook at https://www.facebook.com/amy.f.koko, where she will always follow or friend you back.

Acknowledgements

Many thanks to my sister Cindy for reading and answering every email with, "Please read and tell me if this is funny," in the subject line

Thank you to my sister Valerie for buying me my first laptop and saying, "Stop lurking on Facebook and write something"

Thank you to my coach and mentor Theo Nestor for: 1. Inspiring me with her writing 2. teaching me how to Skype and 3. holding me accountable

Much appreciation to my parents who never doubted me

Thank you Michael for helping me find new love, and new life in a home by the sea

Finally thanks to my children, because I freaking love you guys=

Dedicated to the women who are facing divorce, menopause or both. Fix yourself a cocktail and get on with it. I promise you this: You're going to be fine.

There's Been A Change Of Plans

A Memoir about Divorce, Dating and Delinquents in Mid-Life

Amy Koko

Chapter 1: The Announcement

"I fell off my pink cloud with a thud."—Elizabeth Taylor

I'm standing in my laundry room, admiring my two new front loaders. As washers and dryers go, they're beautiful. So happy I decided on the stainless and not the white. Awesome.

Isn't this what every Jewish wife dreams of? Gorgeous stainless steel appliances in the home of her dreams—in my case, a sprawling ranch on the second hole of the Eastlake Woodlands golfing community in Oldsmar, Florida. Here I am, forty-seven years old, just living the dream. Every morning I wake up to sunshine and the sound of golf carts zipping past my house. The neighborhood is, by the way, gated. No riff-raff getting in here, folks. All is calm and serene, except for the occasional excitement that occurs when animal control is called in to remove a sleeping alligator.

As I'm buffing off a smudge on my otherwise pristine washing machine, a hulking shadow darkens the room and I see a funhouse image of a man reflected in my silver beauties. It's my husband, which is very surprising, as I had no idea he knew where the laundry room was. I'm waiting for him to say, "Hey! What are these things?" Instead he says, "We need to talk."

Okay, here it comes. Finally, Italy! Ciao, Bella! For years, I've been saying, whining, begging that we should rent a villa in the beautiful little town of Ravello, a picturesque village near the Amalfi coast. I see myself on a yellow Vespa, cruising into town and stopping in all my favorite markets where the locals know me as "Bella Donna." Sure, why not? I'm buying ingredients that our local "girl" will turn into a sumptuous meal to be served to us and our guests on our balcony overlooking the sea. What? I don't know what guests; other rich Americans who like to eat pizza, I guess. What better way to celebrate twenty-five years of blissful marriage as we take the giant leap into middle age together?

Mark gently takes a white gym sock from my hands and lays it on the dryer. We walk out to the lanai, which is what us Florida people call the patio. As we sit down on our reclining chaise, I can't help but admire my beautiful outdoor furniture and immediately my eyes focus on the empty section I have reserved, in my mind, for an outdoor kitchen. Is there room for a pizza oven? Instantly, my mind goes off on another tangent, already planning my Italian-themed dinner party, where I will serve my friends homemade pizzas as I regale them with the itinerary of my upcoming trip. Then I remind myself how lucky I am. We have worked long and hard for twenty-five years. There were days when we couldn't afford pizza, much less a pizza oven. I snap back to the present and prepare for my surprise as

Mark takes my hand. For someone who is about to spring the trip of a lifetime on me, he looks a little down. My heart starts pounding as I listen for the words "Italy," "business class," and "I can't believe how awesome you still look after all these years."

"I've had an affair."

Wait.

What?

Some women were getting, "We're promoting you to partner!" or, "Mom, I've been accepted to Harvard," or even "No one makes a pot roast like you do, hon!" But I had been handed these particular words, and, frankly, I didn't know what to do with them. They floated in front of my eyes like the dust particles that take flight once a year when I clean behind the television. I just couldn't grasp them.

A golfer in green, checkered pants yells "Get in the fucking hole!" only steps away from where I sit.

"With who?"

"She's European."

Well, so what? Technically, so am I. My great-great-grandmother came over from Russia, so that excuse is not gonna fly.

"From Switzerland, actually," he went on, raking his hand through his long blonde locks.

Switzerland? Where does a normal middle-aged man find a woman from Switzerland? He couldn't just bang his secretary like every other man entering the "I cannot believe I am turning fifty and I still sell insurance" phase?

I sit in silent disbelief.

"Where? Where did you meet her?"

"She's a friend of one of the girl's in the office."

"I…is she young? Does she work for you?"

"She's thirty-four and, no, she doesn't work for me. She's a pastry chef."

With that last sentence, I should have known the marriage was over. Let us review. My husband of twenty-five years just told me he's been having an affair. Okay, a little marriage counseling and a second honeymoon in Italy, we're back on track and it becomes a blip on the radar. Totally savable. But let's add an exotic blonde—aren't all Swiss people blonde?—young, eleven years younger than this wife, to be exact, pastry chef, and baby, that's all she wrote. I immediately regret the Weight Watcher's lemon bars I have been feeding him the last few years. This is a man who dreams of éclairs. He now has someone who will not only supply them, she'll bring them into being with her own two hands. Nicely played, Heidi.

He looked at me, tears pouring from the blue eyes I had come to think of as mine, "I don't know what to do."

"Do you love her?"

"See, that's the thing. I told her I did, but I don't think I do."

Um, what do you mean you don't think so? Our marriage of a quarter of a century is on the line here. We basically grew up together. We have a lifetime of shitty college apartments, dinners of white bread and A1 sauce, first real paychecks, first homes; first cars with zero miles. We have four children. We have a fucking family, for God's sakes! Tell me you don't *think* you like the paint color in the bedroom, or you don't *think* you want pasta for dinner. But really, I need you to be a little more certain with this particular issue.

"How long has this been going on?" I ask.

"About a year or so."

A year or so…let me think back to what was going on with this family a year ago. If I recall, at that time I was completely obsessed with picking out granite for my new Florida kitchen. For years, I had dreamed of it, granite countertops in Flaaareeed-aaah. When the opportunity came for Mark to take over a thriving business in Florida, I jumped at it. It would mean uprooting four children and a hundred and fifty-pound English Mastiff, but it was a chance for us to have the life we—I—have always dreamed of.

After weeks of trekking through every granite yard in a sixty-mile radius, I had decided on Persian Pearl. And I ordered miles of it. Looking back now, I did find it odd that Mark didn't even flinch at the bill, or at the fact that basically every surface in the house was covered in this very expensive rock. The only thing missing was Pebbles and Dino.

For the first time in a long time, I took a good long look at this man of mine. I noticed his hair, something I grew more and more proud of as the skulls of my friends' husbands became increasingly visible. As they grew balder, my husband's hair was blonder and longer than usual, sort of a mix between Fabio and Prince Valiant. I pictured young, Swiss hands running through it. Sure, I had noticed he'd started buying himself fancy boxer shorts, as opposed to the three-pack from Target I stuck in his Christmas stocking every year, but I guess I just didn't put two and two together.

Sitting there on my new wicker chaise, it all started to make sense. We had recently celebrated our twenty-fifth wedding anniversary and by celebrated, I mean he ate a rib-eye at Capitol Grill while I cried tears on the pink heart confetti that had been sprinkled all over our table in honor of the occasion. I had asked him if he liked my dress and he looked across the table at me, mid-bite, and said, "It's not my favorite." The lobster mac and cheese that I had just forked into my mouth became a cement ball that lodged itself somewhere beneath my left boob and my belly button, making me wish I'd been honest with myself and purchased the large Spanx instead of the medium.

I remembered a few weeks ago finding a pair of women's glasses in his car. When I asked him about this, he told me he borrowed them from a restaurant and had forgotten to take them off. This from a man who would let me bleed out on the bathroom floor rather than risk being seen buying a box of Tampons.

So there it is.

"I'm sorry. I'm so, so sorry," he sobbed. "I'll do whatever you want, but I love you. I'll leave if you want, but I want to stay. I want us to try again."

"I need to think," I said. "I...need to think."

So, here's what I think. I'm forty-seven years old and staring into an abyss filled with my sister and me living side by side in a fifty-five plus community, texting each other pictures of our cats. Neither of us owned one currently, but from where I stood, it was just a matter of time. I envision Saturday night early-bird specials with my parents in Sarasota. I see myself taking half-eaten sandwiches home for later and my purse filled with sugar packets stolen from restaurants. I'm wearing a housecoat. Oh my God.

Okay enough thinking. There was only one thing to do. I had to save my marriage.

"I don't want you to leave," I answered. "I want us to start over and make it work. We can go to marriage counseling and get help."

"I'll do whatever you want," he said.

I spent the next few days looking for marriage counselors and my life revolved around googling "Infidelity +WHY? WHY? WHY?"

This was what I kept asking my husband and myself. The shock had worn off and had been replaced with an agonizing sickness in the pit of my stomach. I was maniacally obsessed with the whole affair thing. It could hit me at the weirdest times. Once I was mid-overhand smash on the tennis court when I put my racket down by my side and told my partner "I have to go." I needed to go home and read more, get on chat sites, look for websites that could just tell me WHY. When I asked Mark, he was no help at all. He would answer with the age old, "It's me, not you. You're a wonderful person." Typically after one of these informative discussions, I would wake up in the middle of the night to find his side of the bed empty. "Where are you?" I would demand by cellphone at 1:30 am.

"I couldn't sleep. Out driving listening to satellite radio."

"Oh, Okay then. See you in a little while."

Stop looking at me that way. Don't you see I had to believe? If I didn't believe that he was out driving around listening to the "Swinging Seventies," I would have to assume that he was still seeing his Swiss baker, and then I would have to tell him to leave, and I would probably have to get a divorce, and then where would I live and who would pay for all my stuff, and that's not to mention the four other people—our children—who counted on us to be a couple.

So, I gear up into saving mode. This involved me standing in front of a mirror, hours at a time, trying to figure out what actually *could* be saved. I took in my new short haircut. Was I imagining this or did my ears suddenly get huge? Was that a crevice beginning on the top right corner of my upper lip? What was the deal with my eyebrows? Where did they go?

Let me say here that a lot of us mid-life women do this, sometimes on a daily basis, and then maybe, we put on an extra layer of foundation, and treat ourselves to a new pricey lipstick. We may walk away from that mirror, somewhat dismayed but thinking, "No problem. Nothing an upper body Spanx can't fix." However, in my case, with a thirty-four-year-old blonde, from Switzerland yet, looming behind me, it was much like The Wicked Queen looking into the "mirror, mirror on the wall" and seeing the reflection of that cute and perky Snow White smiling back at her. Unfortunately, this was going to take much more than new lip-gloss and a body girdle. Sorry, Sara Blakely, but let's call it what it is.

A few weeks after Mark's proclamation followed by his tear streaked promise that the affair was definitely over, I found myself reluctantly coming out of the depths of glorious anesthesia, after undergoing what is referred to as a mid-face lift, which is when the doctor basically takes your cheekbones and attaches them to your ears. I can tell you this: It fucking hurts. A lot. You may be wondering what possessed me to take such drastic steps. Here's what I can tell you: Every time I looked into the mirror, I did not see a face. What I saw was lines. I saw imperfections. I saw tired eyes and an old used up wife. I just couldn't get past it. I emptied out my little savings account. Money I'd squirreled away by getting cash back every time I bought groceries. I'd always thought I would use it towards my daughter's wedding dress, or maybe giving my kids a little money towards buying a home when they married. Eww. Notice how all my thoughts were focused on someone's marriage? I gave it all to Dr. C. so that he could make me young again. Trust me when I tell you it's a temporary fix, and, worse, now what I saw in the mirror was a used up wife who had staples in her head.

I returned home and retreated under a hooded blue Snugly, creeping around like a monk who had had the shit beaten out of him. Upon my triumphant homecoming, my hubby had two things to say: 1. "I hope you didn't do this on my account," and 2. "We're out of milk." My face was literally pounding every time I shut my eyes or tried to move my head from side to side. I looked sort of like a bruised ET.

When I finally felt that the healing process was well underway and that I could appear in public without getting the kind of stares reserved for say, someone giving birth unexpectedly in the mall or Oprah in that afro wig, I ventured out. I was greeted by my yard man, Ernesto. With tears in his eyes he said, "Ohhhh, poor lady. Wha happened, lady?" Clearly, my mid-face lift had not taken effect yet.

I persevered, however, and drove myself to the mall for the next step on the "Saving my Marriage" route, Victoria's Secret.

This is where I came face-to-face with the fact that the cause of my imploding marriage might just be my period underwear. Most likely, the nursing bras I still wore occasionally were not my friends either.

Okay, you're right. Perhaps I should have taken time throughout the years to occasionally purge my underwear and lingerie drawers and refresh them with lacy bras and panties that hit somewhere below my rib cage. The thing is, after spending my day checking homework, making dinner, and doing laundry, when I finally get a moment of free time, the last thing I want to do is try on bras at Macy's, which is second only to trying on swimsuits on my things-that-make-me-want-to-roll-up-into-a-fetal-ball-in-the-corner-of-my-living-room list.

Let me redeem myself here by saying, in my mind, some things are just "givens." I'm married to this man, so it's a given I can wear comfortable underwear. I'm married to this man, so it's a given that he'll be understanding if I want to watch *Breaking Bad* instead of sex. I'm married to this man, so it's a given that he'll not be screwing blonde pastry chefs without my consent or knowledge. See? This is my thought process.

Anyway, I walk into Victoria's and am immediately greeted by a table full of what they call panties, but what I call thread. So this is the thong underwear everyone's been talking about? What's the point of wearing them? My biggest fear is I will forget I have them on and they'll eventually disintegrate and melt into my vagina, immediately causing cancer cells to start forming. Honestly, I don't get it.

Remembering that I'm here on a "Save My Marriage" mission, I pick out three pairs: one white, one red and one black lace. I have to admit, I did feel sort of sexy walking around with a bag full of underwear that's not meant to keep a sanitary napkin from popping out the front of my pants. I began to think that maybe saving my marriage was really doable.

On the advice of Dr. Judith our marriage counselor, we purchased the book *The 5 Love Languages*, which espoused the following: *What if you could say or do just the right thing guaranteed to make that special someone feel loved? The secret is learning the right love language!* I began to realize that "Oh shit, I'm out of Tucks" and "Jesus! Courtesy flush please" may not be making my special someone feel loved. I started softening my tone and using the word "honey." I ended every phone call with a cheery "Love you!" I basically became June Cleaver, spending my day waiting for Ward to get home so I could tell him, lovingly of course, the funny things that Beaver said to Ms. Landers today. Bear with me, I was really trying.

At night, I would hit the sheets with my throbbing cheeks, lacy nighties and useless ass thread. Lying beside Mark, I would turn to him and silently cry, "Want me!" Sex was still infrequent at best, and I blamed that on the obnoxious crying and sniveling that poured out of me anytime we attempted to be intimate. During these times, I tried to let go and be carried away in the moment, but low and behold my mind would not cooperate and the silent litany would begin to play: "You are my husband and father of my four babies. How could you have done this with someone else? Did you say these words? Did you put your hands here? Does she know about the ticklish spot at the base of your throat? Does she love the way your hair clings to the back of your neck as much as I do?" And the tears would just flow. Sort of a downer I guess. Not to mention the endless wedgie that kept me from getting my full eight hours of blissful sleep.

If I may interject a quick side note regarding sleep and mid-life here, and I may, as it's my book and let's face it, really, who's gonna see it other than my mom and sisters? I definitely don't want my dad seeing the whole crying sex thing.

Sleep for a mid-life woman goes from being something she does at night for mental and physical health reasons to her whole reason for living. It's what makes life worthwhile. Forget kids. Forget chocolate-espresso gelato. Forget wine. Yes, you heard me. Forget wine. Our new goal and aspiration is to be in bed in time for one episode of *Top Chef* before turning out the light and drifting off. Sleep is the carrot dangling in front of our face, keeping us moving through the day, chasing that first crunchy bite. When I am not sleeping, I'm trying to figure out when I can go back to sleep.

The problem is I find the sleep I do now is different from the sleep I did when I was younger. Back then, I would fall asleep curled up on my side like a little baby bunny or perhaps on my tummy with my long hair fanned out all over my pillow, pretty sure my mouth was closed and I was breathing quietly through my nose.

Now, I can fall asleep without meaning to, typically on my back, my mouth open with spittle pouring down my chin. With my new super short hairstyle, I look sort of like my Uncle Paulie, who, when I was little, was always passed out at my grandmother's house after drinking a case of beer and smoking several cartons of cigarettes within a three hour time span. When I asked my mother why he does this, she would quickly lead me away by the arm and whisper, "He was in the war."

Anyway, this is just something to be aware of. Not Uncle Paulie's beer consumption, raging PTSD or our matching haircuts, but the sleeping with the open mouth thing. Unfortunately, all the thong underwear in the world will not help with this particular problem.

The other thing I need to tell you is during this time frame, roughly a year or so, I lost my left ovary and fallopian tube. No, I don't mean I put them in my beige purse then changed over to my black purse then remembered they were still in the beige purse and dumped the whole thing out and they had magically disappeared. I mean a doctor had to go in and remove them. Another reality I faced in midlife is that parts of my body, the good parts that defined the last thirty years of my life allowing me to create and carry children and blow dry my hair without breaking into a drenching sweat, were now signing out and leaving the job site. This was quite a blow to me. Me—someone who could get pregnant just by saying the word baby, give birth, then reapply my makeup and down the New Mothers' Surf and Turf dinner within a three-hour time span.

The pain in my lower left side began as a slight twinge and crept up on me slowly. For a while I was able to ignore it and focus on my icing my throbbing face, trying to remember to remove invisible thong underwear, and speaking the language of love to a man who was constantly looking down at his cellphone. Then the blood came and I knew it was something that needed tending to.

Two ultrasounds, one cat scan and one professional diagnosis of Raging Cancer Phobia later, it was determined that due to having my tubes tied fifteen years earlier, the offending tube had filled up with fluid, married itself to my ovary, and they had then invited my bowel over to hang out. It all had to be removed.

In and of itself, removing a fallopian tube and ovary is really not a big deal. You still have hormones, you still have those fabulous periods, and it's outpatient, for God's sake. For me, however, it became another reason why my husband didn't find me sexually attractive. Though he said the affair was over, I thought, how could he not miss her? She still had two functioning ovaries and fallopian tubes that could make egg travel possible. The thing is that while my husband was out fucking a woman twelve years younger than myself, my body was slowly closing up shop. She was lush tropical wetlands and I was the Sahara. Though he professed not to think of her and still tried occasionally to make love to me, I felt old, ugly, and unbearably depressed. And scared. I felt very scared.

Months had passed since the announcement, and I still felt her between us. The marriage counseling was somewhat helpful, until he was home late from work or had to stay one extra night on a business trip at the last minute. Had he always gone out for a Starbucks on Sunday nights? Should I be pleased or concerned that he now carried two cellphones so that the kids and I could always reach him at the new number? Basically, I was a forty-seven-year-old woman walking around with one ovary waiting for my vagina to dry up and knowing that my husband had tasted sex with a ripe, golden woman coated in flour and sugar.

Okay, I wasn't going to tell you this because this book is not about bad things my ex-husband said to me and in fact this is the one of the few chapters focusing on my divorce. But I need you to know where I was coming from at this point in my life. From time to time, I would have major crying jags and demand answers from Mark that he wouldn't give me. I would repeatedly ask about the sex. I wanted to know everything. He wouldn't tell me. No amount of screaming, crying or flailing my fists on his chests would get him to crack. Looking back now, I thank him for this. However, one time I asked him if she had ever seen me. He became very quiet and looked down at the floor. I knew immediately she had.

"Tell me," I demanded.

"She saw you one morning out walking Rudy. She was following you."

"What did she say?" I breathed.

Several seconds passed before his eyes met mine and he answered, "She said you looked like an old hag."

The room began to spin, and I nearly fell to my knees. My gut reaction was to agree. However, in my defense, is there anyone who looks good on their early morning dog walk? I mean, typically I am wearing fashion boots, pajama pants and an oversized sleep shirt and ball cap. I may be chewing camel-like, on a rolled up strawberry fruit snack, my daily breakfast appetizer. I really have to call it here: "No fair! Do over!"

Looking back now, I have to wonder why in the world would he tell me that? In any case it became clear to me at that moment that: 1. I needed to rethink my dog walking outfit and, 2. I had to see her.

Chapter 2: Seeing Is Not Believing

"Enemies are so stimulating."—Kathryn Hepburn

What started as a tingly prick of curiosity quickly became an all-consuming need to lay my eyes on this flour-throwing beeeyach who couldn't even cut me some slack in the pre-coffee hours. Also, I was beginning to suspect that she might not be a nice person. I, for one, feel that when you're married lover asks, "So, what do you think?" after you've successfully stalked and then followed his clueless wife down the street, you use a bit of decorum when answering. I'd have said something along the lines of, "She's lovely. Not many women could pull of that fashion boot-pajama pants look, but she really owns it," or, "She's so brave. I would never have the guts to walk down the street like that." But, that's just me. My mother taught me to speak like a young lady and I usually try to, which is why I never use words like "cunt" or "twat" and would rather you not use them around me, either, because they're filthy and gross. One time I was out with a new friend whom I was really starting to bond with, i.e., obsess over. We met at a school luncheon. She had a great haircut and was carrying one of those big Louis Vuitton purses that made her look extremely chic, but made me look like I need to go store my luggage until my room is ready, and so I liked her.

Sitting down for lunch at a local seafood establishment, I was working up my nerve to invite her and her husband over for dinner, when all of a sudden she looked over at the table next to us where a young man had just been served the Grouper Special. "Oh My God," she said, "That smells like a dirty twat."

I was distraught by her words, not only because I was planning to order the Grouper Special, but also because I knew our blossoming friendship was over. I could never take her home to my mother. I ordered the blackened salmon and that was that.

Anyway, this obsession with getting a look at this other woman was beginning to eat up the better part of my days. Finally, with just a little bit of creative investigation, I managed to uncover her name. By a little bit of investigation, I mean I went through every pair of pants and even shirts with pockets in my husband's closet. I emptied out his nightstand drawers as well as the Tumi shaving kit he used for traveling. I lifted up the mats in his car and sorted through each minuscule scrap of paper in his glove box. I checked the history on his GPS and maniacally drove to an address I didn't recognize just to find myself in front of the new local donut shop. Six glazed cream-filleds later, I was still no closer to discovering her name.

Finally, I tackled his home office. I emptied out every drawer and every cabinet. I even sorted through the shredder looking for...what? I don't know. A perfume scented scrap? What the hell? Then I opened the bottom drawer that I never pay attention to because it sticks and makes a horrendous squeaking noise. Pay dirt.

Lying right there was a black, soft covered datebook. Written on the inside cover in bright red ink was a woman's name with a ton of vowels. Now she was mine.

Of course, I have no intention of revealing her name. In this publication, she will simply be referred to as OW, which of course stands for Other Woman, not Old Whore like you thought.

I raced to my computer with my new information and typed her name in, my heart beating faster than my fingers were flying. The only thing that came up was a folk singer in Sweden. I tried Google images, and the same folk singer appeared. Unless Mark had developed a penchant for women in their sixties with long gray hair and dark John Lennon glasses, I didn't think this could be her.

Then I went into the white pages and there I found that for $47.99 I could get an entire background check, complete with phone number and address. Within seconds, I had what I needed. OW had an ex-husband and a daughter who was seven years old. More importantly, I now had a phone number and an address. Instantly, I was in my car with this address programmed into my GPS. This can't be right, I thought. It says total travel time is ten minutes. Basically, I took three right turns and then I was in front of her house. That cunt! Yes, Mom, you heard me. She lives right next door to my bank. Our bank!

Oh my God! Did the tellers know? Did they all talk about me after I deposited my weekly household budget check and threw a handful of mints into my purse? This was too much. She was literally part of my day-to-day world. I might even have run into her and didn't know it. I tried to think back and remember if I had seen any Heidi Klum look-alikes at Publix, the carwash, the nail salon or my favorite wine bar. I just couldn't remember. Disconcerting to say the least.

My other problem was now that I had the information, what was I going to do with it? Was I going to call her up and ask how she was feeling now that she had been cast aside for an old hag who eats rolled up strawberry snacks? Was I going to sit outside her house and then drive away when she came out, like I did in eleventh grade when I had a crush on Mr. Mann, my Sociology teacher?

Uh, yeah, I was actually.

I started slowly riding by her place several times a day, just trying to get the lay of the land. I memorized every window, every door, every freaking blade of grass. The house was unremarkable, painted gray with white shutters and a one-car garage, with a wreath of dried flowers hanging on the door below a sign that said *Welcome.* It looked...normal. What had I been expecting? A broken down hotel on the other side of town with women hanging out the window yelling, "Me love you long time!"? Sort of.

I continued my surveillance for five days driving by about four times a day, but never getting the courage to actually park and wait for a sighting. Finally, on the fifth day, as I turned down the street and began making my way slowly to my target, a little boy appeared and yelled, "Mommy! She's here again!"

A young woman with an apron came running from the house and I realized I had been made. I hadn't counted on nosy neighbors becoming suspicious of a middle-aged woman driving slowly down their street several times a day. I hauled ass out of there before OW came out to find her lover's wife being arrested for pedophilia, right in front of her house.

Obviously, this was not going to work. My private detective days had come to an end, but then I had a brilliant idea. I would hire one—a real one. I began fantasizing about a private dick—hee-hee, excuse the pun—that was the perfect mix between Joe Mannix and Thomas Magnum. These were the men who taught me to kiss. Okay, they didn't actually teach me, but they were the men I thought about when I taught myself to French kiss using the wall behind my bed. Let's not even think about how much lead paint I must have ingested during these tutorials.

Be right back. Must do quick breast self-exam.

Anyway, I saw us meeting clandestinely at a dive bar, where I would be sipping a club soda and lime while Mannix/Magnum tried to talk me into having a dirty martini with him. His handsome face searches mine as he hands over the photos of OW that he has successfully taken without her knowledge. Frank Sinatra is singing, *I've Got You Under My Skin* in the background.

"Your husband is crazy," he says in a deep rumbling voice. "She is nothing compared to you. You are one gorgeous dame." Oh, Joe/Thomas, you are too kind.

Then we would part ways after he made me promise to call him if my marital status ever changed.

Yes, I was actually a little excited about this whole prospect.

For about 20 minutes. My research showed there was no Mannixes or Magnums to be found, just large companies that specialized in criminal background checks and "spouse infidelity," and then finally, one woman investigator. As Mark was friendly with many attorneys and para-military men in the area—don't ask because if I tell you I'll have to kill you—I felt safe going with the woman.

I worked up my nerve and gave her a call. We arranged

to meet, not at a dive bar, but at the new Wawa's that had just opened up across town, which was fine with me, as I had heard their Italian hoagie was awesome. Her name was Donna Ford and I pictured a Mariska Hargitay from *Law and Order SVU* look- alike. I knew that eventually we would become good friends, and I would probably start wearing aviator sunglasses just like she does. Maybe I would even get a license and she and I would go into business together, sort of like a hot version of Cagney and Lacey. Okay, this is good, too.

I arrive at Wawa's and found that there was good news and bad news to deal with. The bad news was that Donna Ford did not look like Mariska Hargitay. Imagine Rosie O'Donnell in a Boy Scout uniform with a crew cut. If you can do that, then you have a pretty good image of Donna Ford.

We sat at a little side table in the dining area and I explained what I wanted from her.

"Don't follow her, don't tail her, or whatever it is that you guys do. I only want a few pictures. I just want to see her. I need to know what she looks like."

"What does your husband look like so I'll know it's him?"

"Oh no, don't worry, my husband isn't with her anymore." I said these words confidently, though my heart took two quick jumps. I went on, "I just want to see what kind of hair she has. Also, be sure and get some full body shots and if you can't get the whole body be sure and get the upper body, unless you feel that I really need to see what's going on in the lower body and then get one of each. Oh, and if you can get a shot of her shoes that would be good. But that's it. Just a few pictures. That's all I want."

We then discussed when this should take place. We decided on two early mornings the following week, very early, as I figured bakers have to go bake bread and scones and muffins and all of that crap for the we-have-real-jobs crowd. I paid her half of her fee and we parted ways.

Oh, and the good news? The Italian hoagie was phenomenal.

I had to go a week before before getting my hands on the pixs of OW. Luckily, my oldest son had gotten himself into a bit of trouble, and I was able to direct my nervous energy into helping him through it. In all fairness, he didn't actually get himself into trouble. I sort of did.

With all I had going on, what with learning of my husband's affair, recovering from very painful cosmetic surgery and attempting to revive my marriage with ass floss and tips from the video, *Come on Baby, Light His Fire,* I had overlooked one of my very important jobs: renewing our license plates. In the past few weeks, James had been stopped several times on his way to school by a cop who apparently had nothing to do but look for ways to make my life just a tad harder. Ass.

Finally, he gave James a ticket that required an appearance in court. Holy shit. Okay, here's the thing: Ever since I saw *Midnight Express* in college, I am petrified of going to jail, and I don't want my babies in there either. There are two things I remember from my college years—the Mexican casserole they served on Wednesdays and Brad Davis wasting away in a Turkish prison. I pictured myself in the Pinellas County jail, my orange jumpsuit stained with sweat and maybe a little pee, eating beans from a tray with a spork and all bloated from not pooping in months. This, of course, all takes place after my strip search. I was panic-stricken.

The morning of the court appearance, Mark asked if I thought I could handle it alone, as he had a meeting he really shouldn't miss. "No!" I wanted to scream. However, lately I was trying to be a good wife, supportive of my husband and a really great partner, so I wanted to appear calm, cool and in charge.

"Sure," I replied. Falling back on my mentor, June Cleaver, I remembered she never made Ward go to Beaver's school plays or Wally's basketball games. "It will be okay. It will be okay," I began telling myself. I mean, what could happen? A slap on the wrist? Maybe a short suspension of his driving license? He's just a baby after all. If all else failed, I would throw myself on the mercy of the court:

"Judge, it's my fault! I found out my husband was fucking a pastry chef and I let everything go to hell! Please take me in place of my baby."

That afternoon, my darling son stood before the judge in his new khaki pants and collared shirt. "This is good," I thought. This will be just like *Scared Straight,* where they show kids the open toilets in the prison cells to keep them from going down the wrong path. It couldn't hurt for him to have a little bit of fear of making bad decisions in the future.

The judge looked down at James from his giant desk.

"Mr. Koko, you are charged with operating a vehicle with improper licensing. You have disobeyed the law."

Oh, fuck. I don't know about James, but I was scared shitless.

"I'm going to give you a choice, son. You can either do thirty hours of community service, or spend fourteen days in the juvenile detention center."

Perfect, I thought. It will do him some good spending time in the hot Florida sun, walking dogs at the humane society, or helping out kids at the art center. This is how a child learns valuable life lessons.

"I guess I'll just go to jail judge."

What the fuck?

I jumped from my seat. "Please, Judge, can we have a minute so that I can get his father down here?"

He peered down at us from his humongous desk, perhaps trying to ascertain if my son was mentally challenged. Finally he said he would give us one hour to discuss these options.

I immediately ran outside with my cellphone. "Get over here now! James is going to prison!" I screamed into the phone when Mark answered.

Thirty minutes later, Mark burst through the courtroom doors and in that moment I fell in love all over again. Here was the man I married—tall, blonde and fearless. I had flashbacks of him hanging around my locker in high school, his long skinny arm holding an algebra book, his smile sweet and toothy when I finally agreed to our first date, a soft serve ice cream cone on the beach. I remembered him clinging to my hand each time I pushed one of our children into life, then years later charging onto a baseball field, lovingly carrying James off after he got hit in the eye with a wild pitch. I saw the day he left for the Gulf

War, tall, strong, seemingly unafraid, as he kissed his wife and babies goodbye. I loved this man and I knew, in that instant, that all would be all right. There was too much here to let go of. Years from now we would look back and thank God we had saved what we had come so close to losing, as we fell into an empty-nest pattern of quiet dinners on the lanai and naked Sunday afternoons watching old movies in bed. Seeing him come through those doors, I felt like Lois Lane after Superman sets her down on firm ground: My hero.

Mark and James approached the bench and spoke with the judge. In the end, much to his dismay, James was sentenced to thirty hours of community service, picking up trash at the local little league field. To this day, he contends he would have much rather spent two weeks eating beans and playing video games in juvenile detention than walking around picking up hot dog wrappers and styrofoam cups.

Anyway, with this crisis averted, three days later Donna Ford and I met across our wobbly table in the dining section of Wawa's. I was giddy with anticipation. I knew that after I got a look at OW, I'd finally be able to put this whole silly affair thing to bed, so to speak, and Mark and I could move on with a new appreciation for our life together. It would probably result in me growing my hair out, wearing push up bras, and God only knows what other fresh hells I would have to endure, but it was worth it.

Donna's hair was stiff with hair gel, and her khaki uniform was crisp and pressed. She had several badges sewn onto the pockets. What the hell were they? Campfire badge? Knot tying award? Scout Leader of the month?

She entered the Wawa's and sat down across from me. She laid a CD on the table. "Did you see her?" I asked, heart banging in my chest.

She looked at me for a moment, then laid her hand on mine. Uh oh. Obviously she was going to lay some very bad news on me, probably that OW is the spitting image of Heidi Klum and that I should stop being a selfish ass, move aside and let Mark live out every man's fantasy of being with a supermodel. Either that or she was going to ask me out.

Looking straight into my eyes, she asked, "Does your husband drive a black Mercedes?"

And just like that, in the dining section of a gas station, the final scene of my marriage faded to black.

P.S.

Okay, I know you are dying to know what she looks like. First off, let me say that Donna Ford had real NSA surveillance tapes instead of the grainy black and white photos that Mannix always carried.

On the bottom of the screen is stamped the date and time, which was 6:42 am. The tape is rolling and for several minutes nothing happens. Then the front door opens and out comes my husband carrying a bag of trash. Seriously? Through the years, I ruined a countless number of shoes carrying kitchen garbage bags dripping with who-knows-what to the outside trash cans.

His hair is wet and slicked back meaning recent shower. That means nudity. That means...well, you know what that means.

He goes back inside and then a few minutes later they come out together. There she is, her long blonde—was there ever any doubt— hair wet and tangled, wearing a T-shirt and—mom jeans. Yes, mom jeans! High-waisted with a belt. Who puts on a belt at seven in the morning? I haven't worn a belt since ninth grade. Obviously, she is extremely uptight and anal.

Next she goes back into the house while he opens the garage and fiddles around with his car lock. Then she reappears holding two mugs of coffee and kisses him on the cheek as she hands him one.

More than the wet tangled hair, even more than the sex that has obviously just taken place…it was the intimacy of an everyday moment, her knowing what he likes in his coffee and caring enough to make it for him that brought me to my knees.

I watched that video over and over until my best friend took it from me and locked it away in her linen closet, where it resides today.

Chapter 3: Keeping the Home Fires Burning

"I know God would not give me anything I can't handle. I just wish he wouldn't trust me so much."—Mother Teresa

The writing is on the wall and the husband is out the door. There is only one thing to do. That would be walk around in my blue Snugly carrying a box of crunchy cereal. My debit card is on the counter so that my children can order pizza, Chinese, or apparently hundreds of dollars-worth of clothes from UrbanOutfitters.com. I just cannot seem to pull it together. On an up note, however, I have discovered the DIY television station, and although I cannot get myself showered and dressed, I can build a lamp. So there's that.

Yes, of course I know I have to pull it together for my kids. As I mentioned before, there are four of them, two boys and two girls, ranging in ages from thirteen to twenty-two, and let me say here, I may be a shitty wife, which, by-the-way, was news to me and talk about finding out the hard way, and a so-so tennis player, as during our last match my partner yelled, "If you're not gonna help me then get off the court," but I'm a damn good mother.

When Mark had just graduated college and I was the ripe old age of twenty-four, something came over me and I wanted a baby. Let me rephrase that. I *needed* a baby. I was literally, physically aching for a baby. One night I sat down and told Mark what I was feeling and three minutes of young married sex later, I was pregnant with my daughter.

Let me tell you what it's like to be the first of three Jewish daughters pregnant with her first baby. Suddenly, you are Princess Diana, and your mother is calling you every day reminding you that "Anything can happen in the first three months so let's not tell anyone quite yet," which is great for a young pregnant woman already battling severe cancer phobia and an intense fear of armed burglary. I basically laid on my couch for three months afraid to move. Then during my fourth month, to reward myself for keeping my baby alive, I began wearing maternity clothes, which I really didn't need yet, and walking around holding my belly while leaning backwards the way pregnant women do about five minutes before they give birth.

Mark looked at me one day as I was making my way to the kitchen.

"Why are you walking that way?"

"Uh, because I am a pregnant woman? Because I have a baby growing in here and my back hurts?"

"Okay, but you can't even tell yet. That must be some baby!"

Sure, I milked pregnancy for all it was worth. Sometimes I would be sitting on the couch watching television and look at Mark and say, "I need a kiwi. Now." Ten minutes later, voilá, there it was. I loved every moment of being pregnant, and, I have to say, it was a time I was truly at my best. For me, the perks were amazing. It was the only time people ever told me "You need to eat!"

Labor, of course, was another story. I went into labor during an episode of *Miami Vice* and this was before TIVO so I was really bummed that I would have to miss a whole episode of Sonny Crocket. Mark and I called my parents, told them we were going to the hospital and to please pick up Yoda, our Pekingese, as back in those days you stayed in the hospital for three days learning how to diaper the baby. Even though Mark would be returning home in the interim, he was not a dog person, which could mean Yoda would be a dried up skeleton lying in his own feces by the time I returned home. Shortly after I was put into a hospital bed and realizing that the only way to make this agony end was to push a person out of my body, my parents arrived at the hospital with a pint of frozen yogurt as my dad has very bad hearing. The nurse rushed it into the delivery room and handed it to Mark who calmly spooned it into his mouth while coaching me through contractions.

Everyone says that a woman has labor amnesia and they forget how bad the pain is so that they will continue to have children. Not so. I remember every minute of those three hours. Jesus Christ. Mother. Fucker. Enough said about that, I think. If you're a mother, you know what I'm talking about and if you're not but are contemplating it, I'm probably just exaggerating for the sake of trying to get published so...go for it.

Scream. Scream. Swear. Swear. Breathe. Breathe. And then...there she was. The nurse handed me this beautiful baby and, in that instant, life changed. I know every mother says that, but it's really true. Nothing matters anymore but the tiny person in your arms. I remember the sweet smell of her head and the instant warmth we generated when I held her against me. How I adore that child and the ones that followed. So, I knew I owed it to them to be the mother I had always been…nurturing, caring, phobia-ridden and still somewhat sane.

My oldest daughter, Mackenzie, had decided to attend a film school in New York City, so only my younger three—James, seventeen; Heather, sixteen; and Gabe fourteen—are privy to my descent into this new *Gray Gardens* lifestyle. I'll be Big Edie, surrounded by squirrels and eating my Saltines while my kids dress up in costumes and sing me songs. From the look of my nightstand full of empty cheese cracker boxes and Greek yogurt containers, I'm well on my way.

And then, one afternoon, I look up from an edition of *House Hunters*, where disgusting newlyweds are looking for their starter home. "Good luck with that!" I yell at the TV as I down the last of my orange Gatorade. "Don't worry about that man cave he insists on. He'll be gone in a few years and you can turn it into a sewing room."

In the doorway stands my sister Victoria, who flew in from New York City, apparently summoned by my mother, who could no longer stand my daily crying jags while she was trying to enjoy her morning coffee and raisin toast.

First of all, what is it with people from New York City? They carry themselves like super-heroes, wearing all black. Nothing fazes them. They're always dressed like they stepped out of a magazine. They act like wherever they are is where they're supposed to be, so unlike myself, who can wander around the Publix parking lot for hours looking for my car. Sometimes I find myself wondering, "Wait a minute...did I walk here?"

Second of all, how did Victoria come to be an amazing professional, dressed in black and living a glamorous life in New York City, while I'm a sniveling lump on a couch in Oldsmar, Florida? She is three years my junior, but definitely the adult in our relationship. I went off to college to study communications, like everyone else in the late seventies, and ended up at North Texas State because I was obsessed with the TV show, *Dallas,* and they accepted me. In my one and a half years there, I learned to do the Cotton Eyed Joe and ran around wearing cowboy boots, which made me feel less of a Jewish girl in a bodunk town in Texas and more like Lucy Ewing. Then one day I was walking to Spanish class where I would be sitting through a test that I had not studied for…and besides, who needs to learn Spanish? Like *that* would ever come in handy. I turned around, walked to the finance office and dropped out. Of course, it was two days after the cutoff to get a refund on the out-of-state tuition my father had just paid, proving once again my knack for perfect timing. I called Mark, who was stationed at Ft. Bragg, told him we were getting married and then called my father to drive down from Louisville and pick me up. He was less than pleased, but I give him credit. He came.

So, basically, whereas I spent my college years line-dancing and attending Pi Kappa Alpha chili cook-offs, VVictoria spent hers studying and interning for the local television station covering sporting events. Fast forward to her job today, with a major network producing music videos. Up to now, she's won five Emmys, which for some reason, are stashed away in her linen closet. I still have my participation award from the neighborhood tennis tourney on the mantle, so I don't really get it.

Anyway, she approaches my kitchen/bed and says, "Get up."

"I can't. I just really can't. I don't want to."

"Well, you don't have a choice. I can only stay two nights and mom wants me to take her to Costco tomorrow, so today is the day."

After much urging, I stumble into the shower. When I come out, Victoria has assembled an outfit for me and laid it on the bed. I put on the jeans and T-shirt and go to stand before a mirror.

"You need a belt."

At this time in my life, the concept of a belt was on par with the concept of solar power windmills. A belt was part of a life in another galaxy, where I had a husband and couple friends and date nights on Saturdays. In this galaxy, all that was required was a pair of sweatpants with a pull tie waistband.

Once I'm dressed, she leads me to the kitchen table, which is covered in McDonald's bags, empty Chinese food containers, and paper plates with pizza crust remnants. "Look," she says, "It sucks. It's horrendous. He is a horrible person. A goddamn son of a bitch, even. But you have kids and they need you. So get your shit together."

Surveying my surroundings, I know she is right. Although I was getting a lot of gratification from drunk texting, sending Mark daily emails all ending with the word *motherfucker*, and riding around with my car windows open listening to Carrie Underwood's *Before he Cheats,* I knew I was not getting what I needed to help me with this process. What I needed was a divorce attorney.

Years ago, when I moved to a new town, a good friend told me how to find a new hair stylist.

"Ask people with good hair who they go to, and when three people give you the same answer, that's your guy."

I wondered, does the same thing apply to divorce attorneys? Do I wander up and down the aisles of Publix until I spot a likely candidate? "Um, excuse me, ma'am, I see that you have a bottle of Alice White chardonnay in your cart and nothing else, are wearing a baseball cap and look completely miserable. Could you perhaps recommend a good divorce attorney?"

Victoria and I do a Google search. After extensive research and two number fives from Jimmy Johns, we narrow our search down to two well-known attorneys here in town—Judith Friedson and Madison Pierce. Judith looks like a Judith. She has an A+ reputation and is known for causing grown men to cry for their mommies during mediations, but I fall instantly in love with the name Madison Pierce. She was the girl in high school who was rushing off to cheerleading practice while I was rushing off to the orthodontist and Home Ec club meetings. I loved just saying the name as in, "Oh yes, I'm using Madison Pierce," or "Perhaps you've heard of Madison Pierce? She's my attorney," as if I owned her. She had me at Madison.

I promise Victoria I would phone Madison within the next twenty-four hours, after politely declining to join her and mother at Costco the following day. Watching my mother peruse the aisles of ten-gallon jars of artichoke hearts and keg-like barrels of Worcestershire sauce was probably all it would take to finally push me over the edge.

On the day of my scheduled meeting with MP, I feel large and in charge as I drive to her office. I know that Madison will lead me out of this dark hole victorious, with private pilates sessions still intact and my monthly coloring at AVEDA hair salon still on the books. We'll celebrate together over dirty martinis at Capital Grill. Over time, we'll become besties and probably have girls' weekends at some fabulous South Beach resort. I'm feeling really good about this.

While waiting in the outer office, I make myself comfortable on the sleek microfiber, steel-colored couch. Of course, Madison would have contemporary and sparse surroundings; she didn't need clutter and stuff. I check out the titles of the books that had been placed on the coffee table for my perusal: *Getting Out and Getting On* and *The Official Guide to Dating Again.* Across from me on a black leather armchair was a throw pillow that said, "Eat, drink, and remarry." How clever is my Madison?

Finally, I'm led into the inner sanctum. Behind a desk the size of an Army tank, all chrome and glass, sits Madison Pierce. Sunlight bounces off mirrored tiles above the wet bar and creates a halo affect around her. My eyes have a little trouble adjusting to the light, but I can make out a sleek, auburn pageboy haircut, diamond encrusted readers that I just know are from a real eye doctor and not CVS, and long red fingernails. She leans back into her chair and says, "So? Tell me."

Suddenly, my tears begin to fall, my nose is running and I am snorting like a pig. She pushes a box of tissue towards me and I can tell she is sort of grossed out, and maybe a teensy bit bored. I tell her the story of the young baker from Switzerland who stole my husband and my perfect life.

"Did he buy her a car or any other property?"

"No, I don't think so."

"Well, then, in this state she's irrelevant."

Hmm, this was not going as I had planned. I had expected her to jump from her chair and yell, "The injustice of this! I will have her deported, after coming to you on her knees with a sincere apology and a box of the world's most expensive chocolates."

She begins to write out our plan. "We will ask for permanent alimony and try for the house," Yay, Madison! "You will get 50% of all marital assets, and, of course, we will ask for sole custody of the children with free visitation." Umm...yay?

I realize that only two out of the four are under eighteen, but is that sole custody as in I have them all the time? Like every day and night, every meal, every school project that requires a hot glue gun? Every twenty-four-hour stomach flu, every summons from the school principal or possibly the sheriff? That kind of sole custody?

She sets a date for a mediation hearing and tells me to go home and get all my files and paperwork in order.

Problem 1. I don't have any files

Problem 2. I don't have any paperwork

Problem 3. What are you talking about?

It hits me in this moment that I could no longer say, "Oh,

just call my husband. He handles all of that stuff." Mark had handled our bills, taxes and all monetary decisions, while I took care of our vegetable intake, pediatrician runs and choosing a kitchen floor; talents that seem pretty useless at this stage in the game. It's during revelations like this that my anger towards my soon-to-be-ex, referred to as STBX by us divorcees in progress, rears its ugly head and begins to spew from my mouth like pea soup from Linda Blair.

"What the fuck?"

I begin muttering as I wander the halls of Madison's austere office building looking for an elevator, "I am supposed to be in fucking Italy not trying to pull together all my Target receipts! God damn fucker!" Apparently, the security guard thinks my rant is coming from being unable to find the exit and kindly escorts me to the elevator, down fifteen flights and out the door.

"Enjoy your day," he says as he steers me out towards the street.

"Oh I doubt it," I say, "My husband left me for a Swiss pastry chef and now I have to go home and find paperwork."

"Okay. Well, bye now." He retreats inside and I'm sure he's thinking, "Big surprise. Who could be married to a moron who can't find her way out of a building?"

Here's another thing I realize as I exit the building onto the sunny street, gaping at all the people I just *know* are happily married; that I'm not the first woman to get divorced and I won't be the last and, frankly my dear, no one gives a shit. The thing to watch out for at this stage is the people who *pretend* to give a shit, and you know who you bitches are.

For the twenty-two years, prior to our move to Florida, Mark and I had been living in Louisville, Kentucky. We ended up there because my father had an insurance business and when Mark graduated college, I told him I really missed my mom and the ribs at Stanton's BBQ on the Ohio River. Wouldn't it be great to be near family, meaning mine? Of course it would, and I especially pointed out that, as my dad had no sons, someone should be learning the business so that it would always remain in the family. Mark looked down at my flat, pregnant belly, protectively covered by my hand, and a few months later we were renting a house just miles from my parents, where I began nesting like the rat who used to live in the basement cabinet where I kept all my wrapping paper.

Growing up, my children attended private school, because… well, because I said so! And yet reasons for my failed marriage continue to elude me. Most people would agree if you can afford it, there are benefits, such as smaller classes, more intense curriculum and, most importantly, the chance to be a cheerleader even if you cannot do a basic somersault, much less a back-flip off a pyramid made of other cheerleaders. I didn't attend private school, and it's a known fact that Jewish girls don't tumble. So I had to be content with being on the "pep squad," otherwise known as girls with dark hair and braces who will not, in their wildest dreams, ever be cheerleaders. Ever. Dream on, losers.

Was I a bit of a social climber? Well, excuse me for wanting the best for my children, for insisting on a school with manicured grounds and a real life log cabin left over from Abraham Lincoln sitting on the main lawn. Okay. Yes, I was.

Still, even though my oldest daughter, Mackenzie, answered "Oh I don't know. I think they're studying the Civil War or something," when I asked her why there were photos of Hitler in the 6th grade classroom, I still felt my kids were getting the best possible education, not to mention chef-created lunches with a full salad bar. Arugula, I kid you not.

The downside of private school, other than the constant requests for parents to participate in their children's learning— that's what I'm paying you dickweeds for— are the mothers who all looked like Doris Day and wear cardigans thrown over their shoulders even in the summer. They all drive Mercedes wagons with their Coach purses thrown on the front seat, and wear David Yurman bracelets just to drive car pool. My Fossil purse and I just couldn't get through the ranks, even when I did adorn myself with my favorite Swatch watch with the St. Bernard face. I would get invited to parties and feel like I was making headway, only to have the hostess pretend not to see me at the grocery store the following week. It took me a while to realize these were just fundraisers, and as they were not raising much funds from Mark and me, we were not part of the popular crowd. Give me back my David Cassidy haircut and uni-brow and it's seventh grade all over again.

Now, suddenly, these women were appearing out of the woodwork from seven hundred miles away, sending me emails and Facebook messages. "OMG! So sorry to hear about you and Mark. If you ever need to talk I'm here for you."

Thank you so much. What was your name again?

Anyway, enough already. I followed Madison's advice, began getting my meager paperwork in order, took back my debit card, began cooking meals and made myself stay out of bed until at least after dinner. It was during this time that I found my new religion, my beacon in the night, my source of inner strength for these times that tried my soul…a little something called Reality TV.

It started slowly with a weekly episode of *Dr. 90210*. I loved watching Dr. Rey touch ladies' boobs and tell them how he could make them even bigger, make saggier faces tighter, or make their non-existent lips into Platypus bills. Then we would see his wife, who weighed like fifteen pounds and was always sickly, at their awesome house pretending to enjoy reading his annoying three-year-old daughter a story. There was always a little segment on Dr. Rey doing karate in his home gym, which sort of made him appear a little bit feminine. At the end of the show, we see his client leaving her post-op checkup after the big reveal of a new nose, tightened face or two hard balloons attached to her chest. I was totally hooked.

From there, I moved onto *Extreme Makeover*, *Wife Swap*, and *Biggest Loser*. My days became easier knowing that coaches Jillian and Bob would be spending the evening with me, and that at least one of their team members would throw up on the treadmill. Pure magic. Reality television is now an addiction for me, right behind sleeping pills and spicy snack chips.

In the meantime, life was moving on and so was Mark. I had to accept the fact he really wasn't coming back. This was basically hammered into my head one early December morning, when I pulled two Christmas cards out of my mailbox addressed to Mark and OW. Seeing those names side by side, it dawned on me: they are a them now. They have private jokes, plans for dinner, and favorite TV shows that they watch side-by-side on the couch, probably while rubbing each other's feet.

I ran into the house with my heart pounding and angry tears streaming down my face. I frantically dialed Madison's number, telling her assistant it was an emergency and that I needed to speak with her immediately. Thirty minutes later my phone rang,

"Hello!!"

"Hold for Madison Pierce, Please."

Then, a few minutes later…

"Hello, Amy, what is happening?"

"I just got Christmas cards in the mail, addressed to Mark and OW. At my house! This is MY house!!!"

"Well, I'm not sure what you want me to do. I can't control who sends him Christmas cards. I know it's hard, but you need to get a grip. I'll see you at our meeting in January. Have a nice holiday."

Okay. So much for being best friends and wearing matching glasses. Still, I knew she was right. I had to get a grip. No more crying at my friend's dinner table where I'd eaten so many meals, her five-year-old son wandered up to me and asked, "Do you still have a house?" No more drunk e-mails that now, for sure, had killed any chance I ever had at running for governor. From here on in, I would ride the process of divorce, trust Madison to get me what I needed, and look forward to the future. Yeah. That's what I'll do.

Chapter 4: And Now For the News

"That's the news and I am outta here."—Dennis Miller

Looking toward the future is not as easy as I'd hoped. I can't really picture myself in it, because I'm not really sure who I am supposed to be. Not really a housewife, and kind of a single mom? I'm sort of in a mixed up limbo somewhere between June Cleaver and Shirley Partridge, only my kids don't sing. As a matter of fact, my youngest gave up any hope of a musical career after his third grade recorder concert, where during the grand finale of *When the Saints Come Marching In* Samir Patel threw up and it came out all the little recorder holes. The poor little things kept right on playing, but Gabe was traumatized for years to come. I remember sitting next to Mark, who burst out laughing and said, "This is by far the best Country Day school event I have ever been to." I hate to admit it, but the man can still make me laugh.

In any case, it was time to do something other than bitch and moan and try to figure out where the garage light bulbs are. My friends try to be helpful by asking such insightful questions such as, "Well what do you like to do?" or "Isn't there something you always wanted to do?"

Hmmm, something I've always wanted to do? Yes. Meet Princess Diana. Very tragically too late for that. Appear on the Ellen Show and gab about the time I played racquetball with Larry Hagman when I was in college, which I still consider my highest achievement. Not totally out of the realm of possibility, I guess. Shop in one of those boutiques where you sit on a chaise lounge and the sales consultant brings you the perfect dress, tea in a rose-covered China cup, and finger sandwiches. All certainly lofty goals worth pursuing; however, I realize I need something to do in the meantime or else I'll end up like Snow White, waking up in the morning and heading out to the back yard wearing an apron, where I will sing to all the animals while birds come and perch on my head.

I do some inner soul searching and come up with the idea of volunteer work. Certainly a woman like myself, one who spends most of the day looking at crock pot recipes and then wondering if she should go to Target and buy one, would have much to offer. The question is to whom? Volunteering at the kids' school is totally out. The last time I did that we went to the Science Museum where I was left sobbing hysterically after watching a documentary on elephants. Did you know they physically grieve when one of them dies? Oh my God, don't get me started. All this while little Jordan Bancroft ran repeatedly through the bubble machine because I had forgotten to give him his lunchtime dose of Ritalin.

Think. Think. Think! I tell myself, think back to that day roughly thirty years ago when you made that brilliant decision to drop out of college. What was your career goal? What was it…what was it...oh yes, I wanted to be a TV anchorwoman. Now it's all coming back. How could I use this to help me out now? Maybe I could volunteer at the local TV station and then after a few days of hanging around, bringing local anchor Al Rochelle coffee and bagels, I would get discovered and maybe start on air doing the weather and then move on to the anchor desk, and eventually Diane Sawyer would see me and invite me to New York City to hang out, just us two anchorwomen out on the town. Finally a realistic goal.

After arranging an interview with the woman in charge of volunteers at the ABC affiliate here in Tampa, I am officially slated as a Call Receiver for the Problem Solver. Basically, people call in with complaints about local businesses and the Problem Solver goes to the business, thinking that if she keeps this up, eventually she will be discovered by Keith Morrison on Dateline, and gets the business owner to fix the problem, and then everyone shakes hands on the air. My job is to screen the calls and figure out which ones deserved to be put on the Problem Solver's desk, worthy of airtime and possible Dateline recognition.

On my first day, I'm taken to my very own cubicle with a real desk and beige chair on wheels and a phone with a ton of light up square buttons. All around me people are answering phones and speaking very seriously into them. My guide, Beatrice, and, yes, she looked like a Beatrice, sort of like Aunt Bea from Andy Griffith, tells me this was a job—Um, no Beatrice, you get paid for that— to be taken seriously. She tells me about helping an elderly woman who had been scammed by a computer company into paying three hundred dollars a month for a five hundred dollar laptop computer, and about the young couple who paid a landlord two thousand dollars for a rental home and then the landlord vanished before they ever moved in, apparently taking the keys with him. Finally, I think to myself, my chance to better the world and help people. This is what I was meant to do.

I take a few calls, which are really boring: "The electric company owes me money" and "My son-in-law stole my washing machine." Sorry, white trash family feuds are not my department. By ten o'clock, I'm ready for a break. I go into the break room and fix myself a cup of coffee, then decide to give myself a little tour of the place.

I wander up and down the halls, listening in on conversations and wondering if there were any snacks I had overlooked in the break room. Suddenly, I come to a wide-open atrium and below me there it is: the news desk. Oh my God, I have to do it. I take the elevator down and tiptoe onto the set, which at this time of day is deserted. I approach the desk, pull back the chair and sit down.

So, this is what I had missed. Of course, I have to play the "what if" game...What if I had passed that Spanish test? What if I had graduated college? What if I had become an anchor woman like Elizabeth Vargas but without the drinking problem? What if my biggest problem today was if the color of my blazer read well on camera instead of fearing a run in with my husband's girlfriend at Publix?

For just a moment, I feel cheated. For just a moment. Then I think of my children and know that silly arrests and boring recorder concerts aside, I have something in my life that I truly love, that I treasure. They might not get me on Dateline, although who knows, my youngest has a very explosive temper, but they were my heart and soul and had I gone a different route, I might not have them. While sitting in this anchor chair, my eyes begin to well up and I start digging for my cellphone to call one of them. "Mommy loves you!" I want to yell.

"Mrs. Koko, what are you doing?"

Ugh! Beatrice!

"This area is strictly off limits to volunteers and please remove that coffee cup from the teleprompter immediately! This is totally unprofessional behavior."

Uh, hellloooooooo Beatrice. That's why they call it volunteer work. If I were a professional, I would be wearing Michael Kors heels, carrying a Tory Burch briefcase and telling you to use half creamer and half skim in my coffee.

"Oh gosh, sorry. I got a little lost looking for the restroom, and..."

"There is a restroom right next to the cubicle area upstairs. Really, this is the kind of thing that makes all of us volunteers look bad. Please don't do it again,"

What I want to say is, "Fuck the hell off, Beatrice," but what I do say is, "Okay, Beatrice, now I know."

I return to my cubicle resigned to do my "job" to the best of my ability. I try to remind myself that people are suffering and I have the power to help them. My fellow co-workers are all deeply engrossed in telephone conversations, concerned looks on their faces as they speak in calming reassuring tones. My phone button lights up and I get to work:

"ABC Problem Solver, how may I help you?"

"Uh yeah, I got a guy from the cable company here. He's in my bushes totally naked and I want him outta here before my wife gets home."

"I'm sorry, did you say there is a cable guy in your bushes?"

"Yeah, and he's butt naked and I want him outta here before my wife gets home from work."

Well, seriously? Is there any one of you out there who wouldn't do what I do which is collapse into my chair laughing hysterically? I'm spinning circles in my official work chair, laughing my ass off when Beatrice approaches and asks if we might have a word.

Ten minutes later, I am in my car heading home. It turns out volunteer work is not for me. But then, what is? Suddenly it comes to me—maybe it was time to finish what I had started all those years ago. College! Memories come floating back to me of late night pizza parties and dorm rooms reeking of pot and sex. Of course, I haven't been able to drink rum since that one Halloween dorm party, when I missed curfew and spent the night in the parking lot dressed as a playboy bunny, but let's leave that alone. I don't remember it all anyway.

Yes! This is it. I will go back to college!

I spend the next few days researching my options of local colleges and finally choose a private university about thirty minutes from my house, near a lot of good night life where I figure the other kids and I will be hanging out after classes. Due to certain circumstances, like my advancing age and my barely there GPA, I am advised that I will have to retake freshman English. I'm pretty sure I'll breeze right through that. It couldn't have changed that much in thirty years. A period here, a preposition there...come on. Let me add here that during my first attempt at college, thirty or so years ago, Physical Education was a required class. I ended up taking an aerobics class with some fat girls and three female pre-med students, who I felt sorry for because they always had greasy hair due to studying all night and not having time to prep in the morning with hot rollers and hair spray like us cool chicks. I don't know where they ended up in life, but my guess is not in a freshman English class at the age of forty-eight. I had already decided that if PE was required of me, I would forego traditional college and enroll at ITT Tech where I would pursue a certificate in collision repair and refinishing or become a vet tech. No way was I going to put my knees through that again. Luckily, physical exertion is no longer a requirement to becoming a college grad.

In preparation for my first class, I went out and purchased what I felt to be the biggest necessity for settling into college life: skinny jeans. I pair them up with a graphic T and some supercool wedged heels and know I'm now ready to jump into academics.

The first day of class, I'm beyond excited. As soon as I arrive and park in what I hope is a student spot, I head to the bookstore where I buy several notebooks with the school emblem on the cover and a purple ballpoint pen. From there I head over to the building where I'm to begin my new life as a college coed. As I wander the halls of my new found academia, I feel energized and purposeful. I find my classroom, and stop in front of the door that will lead me to great beginnings. With a deep breath I enter the room, and see about twelve eighteen-year-old freshmen, conversing in some type of foreign language:

"So I was like, Oh my God, dude, you are not putting the bed there, no way. And my roommate was like, yes, I am, and I was like, no dude, no way."

"Dude, Oh my God, your roommate sounds like such a jerk. Seriously."

"I know. Right? Like seriously? I was like, oh my God get over yourself."

Then in unison, "Seriously."

All conversation came to a screeching halt when I enter the room, and I know I have made the right wardrobe choice. It takes me a minute to realize the kids think I am the professor. I take a seat in the front row and realize something else. Skinny jeans slide half way down your butt when you sit down, and your jockey underwear somehow settles in right beneath your boobs.

Things are going horribly awry. It's bringing back the horrible memory of when all the kids were making fun of me at circle time in Kindergarten. It started out as a perfect day when I claimed my independence and got myself dressed without help from my mother. I remember choosing my favorite plaid dress with the velvet black bow and white leotards, which being the forward thinker I am, decided to wear without underwear. Even then I was petrified of panty lines.

I entered Mrs. Chef's class that day feeling like Marlo Thomas in *That Girl*. Young, independent, taking the world by storm. All was going well until we sat cross-legged on the floor listening to Mrs. Chef read, *Green Eggs and Ham.* Suddenly, across the circle, I saw David Lewis pointing at me and giggling. He then nudged Robert Johnson who nudged Barry Carney and suddenly the room was abuzz. Mrs. Chef looked up from *Sam I Am* to see what the commotion was about. Her face turned white as she came face to face with my six year old vagina, which certainly meant no harm and was just listening to the story minding its own business. A trip to the office, where my mother arrived breathless with a pair of my high-waisted cotton undies ensued, and I was not allowed to dress myself again until third grade. As it happens, I pulled the same trick years later at a frat party in college, where the whole thing was actually very well received.

As I reach around to hike up my jeans, the door opens and in walks Professor Clara Gibson. She's carrying a briefcase and a Vente Starbucks and is wearing Sally Jesse Rafael glasses. There's a big C on her cup, which I know from experience means "cream". I like her immediately. I can't wait for us to start hanging out after class and shmoozing over lattes. I'm so loving college!

"Hello class. I am Professor Clara Gibson and this is English 101. I am going to pass around your syllabus, but you will find it when you log in to your student account, and you will be submitting all work, other than your weekly journal, online."

Huh? I just spent good money on notebooks and a purple gel pen. As I pull out my new school supplies, the kids all around me pulled out paper thin laptops from their backpacks. The room lights up like Three Mile Island.

It takes me some time to get into the swing of things, but I find my way. I buy myself a MacBook Pro and higher waist jeans. I learn to navigate the food court that, compared to the food choices available to me during my first go round with college, seems like a small city unto itself. My days are filled with writing and studying. I have a purpose, and I am freaking loving it.

Of course, at times, it's a bit difficult trying to focus on Professor Clara Gibson's lectures on the MLA system, while receiving text messages such as the following:

we starving plz bring home food

we want subway

G says get usual but not toasted

what time you home??????

come on mom please we starving

So after class, while the other kids are running off to Frankie's for beer and hot dogs, I find myself racing to Subway to feed my children, and typically the night ends with:

at subway you want chips?

??

??

nvmd dad took us out

Oh my God. Dude. Seriously?

Honestly though, I love school and more importantly I love writing. Truly, something caught fire inside me, even though it's awkward at times being the oldest one in the class. We had to pick partners for a project and no one picked me. They were all like, "Eww, I don't want that old lady, she probably smells." I am inspired, challenged and for the first time in a long time, sort of happy.

Back on the home front, I'm making giant strides as well. I take charge of the household bills, making sure the lawn guy doesn't blow grass into the pool, and, most importantly, I take charge of the TV remote. Every night is full of my favorite TV personalities that frankly I have come to think of as my friends. Chef Ramsey, or Gordon as I like to call him, housewives from every city in the country, reruns of *Two and a Half Men*…now *this* is living, I tell myself, or as my OB GYN said when I had reached ten centimeters, "Now we're cookin' with gas!"

Yes, in some ways things are certainly looking up; however, in other ways I have hit a bit of a bump in the road. Unbeknownst to me, Mark and OW have recently moved into my neighborhood. They are renting a home around the corner from me in a luxury section behind a big private, wrought iron gate. Please. As if my cleaning lady's friend's friend doesn't know the gate combo and I won't be driving by several times a day. Dream on.

This, of course, leads to several awkward situations. Some mornings when I'm walking Rudy, Mark drives by in the infamous black Mercedes. He passes right by, not even making eye contact and I think, "Oh wow. There goes that guy that cut four umbilical cords from my body and helped me deliver my placentas."

In a way, it feels like an invasion of privacy. I mean, even my haven my port in the storm, aka the Publix deli, isn't sacred. Saturdays is my Publix day. This is the day when they have enough samples set up throughout the store that I can literally make a brunch out of it. On this particular Saturday, I arrive as usual at eleven o'clock, before it gets too crowded and they started cutting back on the sample portions. And, as usual, I am wearing my gray Nike ball cap that, by now, is pretty much molded to my head. I had just stuffed my mouth with a wad of Boar's Head pulled pork and can feel the delicious greasy sauce running down my chin. When I started to make my way to the wine tasting table, I literally bump into OW.

First of all, someone needs to tell her that this is a grocery store, not a garden party. She's decked out in a yellow sundress and her hair is pulled into one of those stylish tight ponytails that makes my head look like a giant egg. She looks at me and I look at her all the while feeling that slimy sauce turning into a huge zit on my chin. She gives me a look that says, "Really? Is it any wonder?" and aims her cart for the organic aisle, with me following closely behind.

Since when did he start eating almond butter? And whole grain crackers? What? She is heading for the organic eggs. The only thing he ever made in a pan was fried bologna on white bread. Is she still with *my* husband? Maybe she found some other woman's husband that likes organic egg white omelets and crackers made of wood.

In any case, this is going to make a great journal entry for the kids in my class. Once a week we pass around our journals, much to my hideous embarrassment as my first entry was devoted to my gluttonous guilt for eating an entire bag of Ranch Doritos, and finally I will have something to write about that might actually bring me some notoriety.

Last week, I read Rachel Fisher's journal entry that went something like this:

So, I'm like which sorority do you think I should go with and Jeannie was like well the Chi Omegas are sort of slutty but have all the hot Pi Kappa Alpha guys hanging around their house and the Tri Delts have a rep for being really nerdy but I heard they usually have some really good weed at their parties so it really just depends on what's most important to you. So, I decided since weed makes me super paranoid, I guess I will go with Chi O.

So as to appear cool and totally down with it, I added a comment at the bottom of the page, "Good choice!"

As far as school goes, I had decided to take both a short story writing course and a memoir course. These classes were actually upper level, with seniors and juniors, kids much closer to my own age, give or take thirty years. I was in awe of these kids. They had read all the classics, knew what prepositions were and their stories were damn good. Their writing was filled with angst and uncertainties. I wrote a story about the time I told my sister to go inside and tell my mother I got run over and how my mom came running out in an apron crying and then started hitting me when she saw I was alive and well. Guess who got selected to attend a writer's workshop at Whitney Lawrence College with famous authors? That's right, bitches. Me.

For one glorious week that June, I lived in my own dorm room with nothing but a bed and a table. Mornings were spent in class and afternoons were devoted to critiques. Sure, the kids ripped me a new one, but still, it was pure heaven. The only downside was having to share a bathroom with a few other girls and being petrified they would think it was me that stuffed up the toilet—I swear it wasn't. This may sound weird, but I couldn't help but think if it wasn't for OW I would probably be at the dry cleaners that very minute, picking up Mark's laundry or picking out new placemats for one of my themed dinner parties. Gosh OW, I thought. I owe you one.

On the second to last night there, I entered the dining room to see all the kids hunched over their trays whispering.

"What's going on?" I asked my toilet mate, who I think may have never learned we don't flush tampons.

"Michael Jackson died," she said.

Suddenly, from open windows all along this grand, elegant campus *Thriller* wafted through the air and for a moment, no one moved. My God, I thought, the end of one era and the beginning of another.

Chapter 5: Help Wanted

"Trust your husband, adore your husband and get as much as you can in your own name."—Joan Rivers

The day had come for my final meeting with my beloved Madison Pierce. This would be when we would sit down and go over my financial settlement, which, frankly, I was looking forward to because I had been thinking of investing in a new energy bar for dogs that I had heard about through some very hush-hush channels. Okay, it was a weird lady who owns four chihuahuas that I met in the vet's office. Also, I had decided that I *would* go ahead and build an outdoor kitchen and pizza oven on my lanai. I mean, just because I'm divorced doesn't mean I don't love eating pizza outside. Yes, I was definitely ready to become fiscally responsible and start a portfolio, whatever that is.

So, this is how the beginning of my financial independence went down:

MP: "You will be receiving an alimony check every two weeks in this amount." She points to a number on the page that was roughly the amount I spend on our household's weekly snack and soda supply.

ME: "Awesome! I guess there is another account set up for me to draw from on other days?"

MP: Laughing as if I had just made a joke and then getting a real weird look on her face when she realizes I didn't. "Amy, this is it. This is what you agreed to. This is your settlement."

ME: "Okay, no big deal. I still have my AmEx black card for emergencies."

MP: "No, you don't. That account has been closed out. We went all through this in mediation. Do you not remember?"

Mediation? Of course, I remember mediation. Doesn't every woman remember the time she came this close to getting put in a choke hold by a cop and taken down to a squad car where said cop carefully lowers her into the car making sure she doesn't hit her head before slamming the door shut? Duh. Of course, I remember.

I remember sitting in a room with Madison and being plied with espressos and chewy candies from a glass vase. A man came in from the opposite room where Mark and his team were sequestered, brandishing a document. He handed it to Madison, who put it down in front of me. "This is your first offer of settlement, "she explained. I took one look at that thing and went completely still. My heart began beating faster and faster, and I could feel fear laced with venom bubbling up in my throat along with, I'm sure, a worsening case of Barrett's Esophagus. I remember my mouth opening and whispering the words,"Mooooother...fuuuucker." And then all hell broke loose. I literally lost my freaking mind and began to scream:

"That fucking mother fucker! I will kill that mother fucker! You fucker! Where are you, you fucker?" Spit literally flew from my mouth, and I imagine I looked like an even more deranged version of Carrie's mother in the original movie when Piper Laurie loses her shit. It was like I had become possessed by Andrew Dice Clay.

The door opened and another wimpy guy with greasy hair and a suit from Men's Warehouse came in and said, "Mrs. Koko, if you don't calm down we're going to have to call the police. You are upsetting the secretaries." At that point Madison stepped in and hauled me out of there, drove me to Macaroni Grill where she ordered me the lunch plate of Fettuccini Alfredo and said, "That went pretty well, I think."

So, yes, I remember mediation.

Looking back, I now realize what had incited me when I looked down at that first offer. It wasn't only the fear of existing on generic Pop-Tarts for the rest of my days, but seeing my life's work summed up at the bottom of a tally column initialed by my husband of almost thirty years. It's like saying "Okay, you spent twenty-seven years with this man. Together you made it through college and a war, after which you held his sweat-soaked body night after night when he woke up screaming from dreams of limbless men. Now, we see here you gave him four children that you devoted your every waking moment and pretty much every thought to, and you also made sure there was a gallon of egg nog on the Thanksgiving table every year, even though he was the only one who drank it. We think that's worth this amount." That is what I had to come to terms with—a monetary value assigned to my life, otherwise known as a divorce settlement. Once I accepted this, the mediation sessions that followed became much less violent.

I explained myself to MP, "I guess actually seeing it on paper makes it look so...little?"

"Well, I've seen worse. I mean I've seen better too, but I have definitely seen worse. You may want to think about getting a job to supplement your alimony."

Hold the phone. What? I have not held a job since 1984 when I was pretending I knew how to do medical transcribing while putting Mark through college. Looking back, I'm sure there are lots of people out there who have been on the wrong meds all these years due to me just sort of winging it when transcribing reports for doctors in a neurology practice. Those poor guys were taken in by some medical jargon I spouted during my interview. How did it not occur to them that I had picked this up while reading self-diagnosis books in a dark corner of Barnes and Nobles? I'm afraid the significant rise in stroke victims in recent years is due to me wanting a job where I could sit down all day and not have to talk to people.

MP went on, "I mean you're going to want to keep busy anyway, right? Look at this as a new adventure and a good way to meet people."

So. That was it. I said my good-byes. First to Mark, in the dark chambers of Judge Rosen, as we hugged each other and cried, each clasping a copy of our final divorce decree. Then, to

Madison Pierce, my house, which I was only allowed to live in until Gave graduated high school in three years, and worst of all, to my college days and my dream of becoming a famous writer whose book gets made into a blockbuster movie all leading up to that shining moment when I meet Meryl Streep and tell her that *Out of Africa* is my favorite movie and that I love her. I just could not afford to continue. Not now anyway. Maybe someday I would go back to academia, but for now, Madison was right. I would have to find some way to supplement my alimony.

Honestly, I had no idea how to go about even looking for work. Newspaper want ads? Do they even still make newspapers? Then, as luck would have it—because if I am not the luckiest bitch on the planet, come on, who is—a friend of mine had a lead on a possible opportunity. Actually, "friend" may be a little overstating the relationship. Perhaps on her end it was more acquaintance than friend and on my end it was more "adoring weirdo but I'm not gay." I met her at Mark's high school reunion where she was accompanying his old friend, and, I don't know about the friend, but I fell instantly in love. She is tall, blonde, plays a lot of tennis and has a job where she bosses a lot of people around, which I don't think she found in the ect. column of Craigslist. It is possible I may be the first Jew she ever met, but I love her all the same. Plus, she makes me laugh that kind of laugh where I sound like a man and tears run down my face. Her name is Whitney, but in my mind I call her Bryn Mawr. I always invite her to stuff and maybe once in a while she comes and I just sit next to her and think, "Oh my God, you are so freaking cool." Anyway, Whitney had a friend who managed an art gallery in the swanky part of Tampa and was looking for a sales associate. She put in a good word for me and AGHL, art gallery hiring lady, called me to set an interview.

I felt pretty good about it until I entered my closet to put together the perfect "first interview in thirty years" ensemble. That is when sheer panic set in. I needed to take myself from college student mom to super hip art sales person. Then I remembered the stylish Kenneth Cole pencil skirt and slinky black t-shirt I had worn to that now historic first mediation. That was my "I am cool, sophisticated and sooo looking forward to being a divorcee" outfit. It would now be my "I am divorced, job hunting and sooo looking forward to my dinners of Oscar Meyer bologna and Publix spring waters" outfit. Still, I was happy with the final product when I added the black patent kitten heeled pumps I had recently purchased at Aldo Shoes and my diamond stud earrings that Mark had given me for our twentieth anniversary.

Here's how the whole thing went down. On the day of my interview, I awoke early, stood outside with my GPS and programmed in the address of the art gallery. I went inside and made coffee. I came back out and rechecked GPS to make sure the address was still in the recently found list. I went inside and showered. Came out and rechecked GPS. Went inside and put on above mentioned outfit, dried hair. Rechecked GPS. Crammed my feet into kitten heel pumps and headed for car. Start car. GPS dead. Run inside and Google MapQuest. Print out directions to art gallery. Sweat starting in butt crack due to hot Florida sun, wool pencil skirt and death of GPS.

Against all odds, I made it to the gallery a few minutes early. It was on a funky street lined with other galleries, some of which had paintings in the window and others that had my sixth grade bedroom furniture outside with a sign that read, *VINTAGE*. It was sort of a fake funk vibe, with the street looking a bit shady and making you want to double check your car lock, but where you also knew that right around the corner were women wearing those flowy linen scarves tied in fancy knots and eating Cobb salads with balsamic vinaigrette on the side.

I entered the spacious gallery with purpose and confidence, despite the sweaty butt crack. A young girl stood behind the counter, covering a painting in brown wrapping paper and masking tape. "Hi," I said in a very professional manner, which I felt was portraying confidence, yet friendliness, yet maturity yet a "Sure, let's hang out after work" attitude.

"I'm here to see AGHL," I continued.

"Oh yeah. Totally." she said. "I'll get her."

AGHL appeared from behind a closed door and, frankly, I

was a bit put out that she had obviously not put as much time into choosing her wardrobe for this momentous occasion as I had. She was wearing jeans and a loose flowing top and what appeared to be motorcycle boots. Her blonde hair fell casually around her shoulders and she had on dangly silver earrings with little beads on them. Did she forget we were meeting today? The good news is I had a leg up on her. I mean, I was dressed like a professional, not a babysitter from the seventies.

"Hi Amy, I'm AGHL." A handshake ensues, and I am surprised there is no mood ring. "We can sit right over here in this corner."

She leads me through a maze of chopped up gleaming white walls all covered in beautiful paintings. I so love it here. I am going to be awesome at this. I love working!

We take our seats on a little bench. "So, how do you know Whitney?" she asks.

"We actually met at our exes' high school reunion. I love her. " Oh my God! Did that really slip out or did I just think it?

"Well, let me tell you a little bit about the job. Basically it's five days a week from ten until six and on some nights we may hold events, which you would have to stay late for, but they are really fun.

"Oh that's fine, I love events!" I pant. "Actually, my youngest is now in high school, so I'm pretty much free to work whatever hours you need," said the worst mother ever in the world next to Casey Anthony, but for a moment I was temporarily blinded by a vision of me drinking champagne at gallery openings and exhibits, where the artist would probably approach me and ask if he could paint me and I would have to politely decline and walk away leaving him standing there breathless and disappointed. Years later I would be walking through a gallery in France and I would see a beautiful life size painting of myself with the title, *ELUSIVE BEAUTY*. So yes, for a moment I forgot I had a teenager who needed his mother around to supply clean clothes, healthy food, and a good reason not to walk around the house firing up huge joints.

"Oh my God, I have two sons as well. Let me show you a

picture." She pulls her cellphone out of her pocket and produces a picture of two little blonde boys in scout uniforms. "This one is six and my big guy here is eight."

"Ahhh," I drawl. "They are adorable! And such fun ages!" Blah blah...when do I start already?

"Yes, they sure keep us busy. Anyway, have you had any experience in the art field?"

"Well, no, not really any hands on experience, but honestly, I wrote a paper on Mary Cassatt once and fell in love with the whole art world. It's so intriguing!"

"Oh, so you studied art in college then?"

"Um no, I actually wrote that paper in high school, but it made a huge impression on me."

"Oh."

Silent pause. Pause. Pause.

"I like your shoes," she said.

"Oh, thanks!" I almost screamed back.

"Well, anyway let me show you around." Finally! I want to start getting used to my new digs.

She begins to take me through the gallery of little dens, some with colorful sculptures displayed pleasingly around the room and others with giant paintings and wall hangings made of woven fabrics. I was thoroughly entranced. It really was a world of its own and it sort of gave me the chills thinking about the unbelievable talent and passion that went into each piece of work.

"I'm going to take you through our latest exhibit, which has gotten quite a bit of press."

We enter a stark white room where there are mummies lying all over the place. Not exactly the kind you see on Discovery channel, more like Cabbage Patch dolls wrapped in toilet paper.

"This is our exhibit reflecting the horrible Sex Slave epidemic. I'm sure you can see the correlation."

"Oh, yes, wow. This is amazing."

Okay, two things. 1. Haven't sex slaves heard of cellphones? Why don't they call for help? 2. What do mummies have to do with little Asian girls wearing stilettos?

"Anyway," AGHL continues as she leads me away from the creepiest thing I have ever seen, "The job pays eight dollars an hour (cha ching!) and I think that covers everything. I have just one more interview for this position and then I should be in touch within the next two days or so."

Obviously by "in touch," she means a phone call to tell me when I start.

"Great, I'll wait to hear from you," wink, wink...which is me saying, "I know you have to go through the motions of conducting interviews, and I'll treat to Starbucks on my first day."

As I headed out the door a young girl with purple hair and a nose ring was making her way in. "Dude." I thought. "So sorry. You don't stand a chance."

As I got in my car I had only one thought in my head: "Nailed it!"

Sadly, four days later, after rebooting my cellphone twenty-four times and nearly wearing out the REFRESH button on my email, I had to face reality. I did not get the job. How is that possible? I did not take it well. In fact, I took it very personally and decided to draft a letter to AGHL to let her know just how confused I was by this appalling turn of events.

Dear AGHL,

I have replayed our interview over and over in my head and frankly I cannot see why you didn't hire me on the spot. You asked me what I thought my qualifications were for this job and I told you: 1. I wrote a paper on Mary Cassatt in high school and 2. I hardly ever cook dinner anymore. So, really, AGHL, I am at a loss here. Did you or did you not tell me you loved my shoes? Did I, or did I not, listen to you blather on and on about your two boys ages six and eight? Remember that part when I said what fun ages they were? Guess what? It's all downhill from here! Just wait until they discover Jack Daniels and Marlboros and combine those two elements with their free period at school. Also, between you and me, you may want to think of playing down the boy scout uniform photos. In my day, wearing that uniform was just another way of saying: "Hey everybody! Come kick my ass!"

I do not want to threaten, AGHL, but I want you to hear this from me. The day is going to come when I am a published author and will no longer be buying my art from the Target sale rack. And, when the people from Elle Decor magazine come over to film me in my beautiful home, they are going to ask me where I acquired all my valuable breath-taking art. And it will not be from the Michael Martin Gallery, AGHL. Then your boss will say to you, "Hey, didn't you have the chance to hire her?" and you will have to own up to your mistake of epic proportions. You will be fired and your two sons will have to go back to public school, where they will definitely get their asses kicked because of their bowl haircuts.

Okay, of course, I didn't send it, but this experience was a real eye opener for me. Finding a job as a midlife woman was not going to be easy, especially with no college degree. For a moment, I let myself feel really scared. I saw just how ridiculous I must have looked in my wool skirt and pumps, an aging librarian as opposed to a young chick with a nose ring who had limitless possibilities before her, a whole life left to live. Aside from realizing that my Aldo kitten heels were only going to take me so far, I realized I might be spending some time at Starbucks on the other side of the counter. And so what? This is the new reality. Like many other women in my position, it was time to get out there and face the freaking world. Scary? Hell yes. Necessary? Absofuckinglutely.

It was back to square one and Craigslist. Since I felt my talents were widely varied and ran the gambit from how to incorporate melted cheddar into any meal to how to use Febreeze when one sock does not make it into the wash, I decided not to pigeon-hole myself into the ADMIN/OFFICE or GOVERNMENT sections. Is this how Whitney Palin got her job? Instead I went for the ETC category. Surely my talents would meet the criteria of one of these fine opportunities. So, let's see:

1. In Home Bedding Inspection Technicians - Huh? Am I

looking for thread pulls in the comforter or what?

2. Adult Softball Score Keeper - At our age can't we just play for fun and exercise?

3. Blonde/Blue eyed donors needed - Damn this brown/hazel eyed head of mine!

4. Irritable Bowel with Diarrhea? Get Paid to Participate – Oh my God, I love diarrhea. Count me in.

5. Part Time Opportunity: Counting Cars - There's one… Oh! There's another one, that's two...

I think you can see where this is going…nowhere good. I needed to work on a list of my strengths and weaknesses and decide what I really wanted from a job. Then I would see where that led me.

STRENGTHS

1. Reliable transportation
2. Good teeth
3. Healthy appetite
4. Don't drink a lot of soda
5. Have set new records on iPad Solitaire

WEAKNESSES

1. Cannot commit to meeting deadlines
2. Cannot commit to meeting goals
3. Cannot commit to meeting expectations
4. Get extremely tired after lunch
5. Pretty sure I am lactose intolerant

WHAT I WANT IN A JOB

1. To get paid
2. To wear awesome clothes
3. To have power lunches where we drink white wine
4. To have something cool to post on Facebook
5. To be out of the office a lot.

Then it came to me—real estate. Of course! What better time to get into the housing market than right in the middle of the worst recession of our lifetime?

A few weeks later, I once again I found myself in school, but this time in a six-week course, which I attended two nights a week. In Florida, you are required to take forty-five hours of class time and then pass the class test before being allowed to sit for the state Real Estate test. Of course, you can also take the class online, but for me, online class is just another way of saying, "Log onto class site, stare at it for five minutes, then go get bag of chips and surf Facebook."

Real Estate school consisted of me and four other women, two middle-aged, one real young and pretty that I hated, and another one who told me, during one of our bathroom breaks, that she was a practicing witch. I tried to be extra nice to her as I didn't want her casting any spells on me that would ward off prospective clients, such as severe halitosis or a weird eye tic.

In the end, I passed the class test and then low and behold, passed the state test on my first try. I was officially a licensed Florida realtor. I pictured myself as a stylish divorcee with a real estate license, wearing beige Michael Kors suits, Tori Burch heels, and carrying a black leather Chanel bag with my many important files. I envisioned myself driving rich couples around to waterfront mansions and magnificent Florida estates on famous golf courses. Of course, they will be taking me out to exquisite lunches of raw oysters and Sauvignon Blanc, while we write up their offer on a million dollar-plus home. I love this life!

Now picture me driving around with my real client, the grandson of a friend of friend of a friend of the lady who takes my order at Subway. I am driving him and his parents, who have recently arrived from Panama, to various senior communities. Our goal is to get mama moved in and settled before the hip replacement surgery. I have explained to Juarez that "fifty-five plus" means that he cannot live there with them, as he is probably only around thirty-eight. He says he is not planning to live there, but watching mama buckle him in, I have a feeling he is lying.

Papa is in the front seat next to me. He eyes me warily from across the console. "This complex is wonderful and has a convenient bus service to all the local medical facilities," I explain.

"Where es your oosbahnd?" Papa demands.

I look at Juarez from the rear view mirror.

"Papa, she has no husband," he says.

"Eh?" Mama wants to be filled in.

Papa fills her in with a rapid fire of unrecognizable words, but which I think translates into "looozaaah."

We arrive and take the elevator up to the unit we will be viewing. I have total clearance from the owner's daughter to go right on in, but still, I begin to sweat as I unlock the door. Ever since I got my license, I have nightmares of entering a domain and finding the people inside, either engaged in sex or taking a shower. Since this is a community of seniors, I can only imagine the horror of either of those two scenarios.

"Hellooooo! Hellooo!" I holler loudly as we enter. I glance around, all seems in order. The pink velour recliners are empty, as is the harvest gold kitchenette. "Come right in," I tell my entourage. "Take your time and look around. I'll be right here in the kitchen if you have any questions." But please don't, I'm thinking, because this is my first property showing, ever, and I'm kind of winging it, so I can venture a guess, but really that's about it.

I set down my purse and have a seat at the tiny kitchen table. I'm staring at the big scuff on my right shoe, when I hear Juarez cry out, "Miss Amy, there is someone here!" Oh my God! No! Why? What did I do to deserve this hell? I stole one mood ring from Sears in 1975 and will pay for it the rest of my life.

I enter the bedroom and I see they are correct. There is definitely someone here. Grandma is sitting upright in a rocker, fully clothed thank the Lord, and is in a condition I believe medical professionals describe as...fucking dead. I'm fighting to maintain calm even though I am so totally creeped out. A dead person? Seriously?

We haul ass out of there like the Scooby Doo gang. I was sure I saw a big green apparition chasing us. I immediately call my office manager and tell her to get in touch with the owner's daughter. Let her know we think mother may be feeling a bit under the weather.

With no invite for Sauvignon Blanc, oysters or even another appointment forthcoming, I drop the Panamanian contingency off at their car. As the day shouldn't be a total loss, I decide to head to Jimmy John's Subs for a Number Five with extra hot peppers. My mouth is watering as I pull up and I grab my purse even as I am still parking. But wait, no, I don't. My purse is not there. Where could I have left an entire fake Michael Kors purse? Then it hits me. It's on the table in grandma's kitchenette. Probably being ripped apart by zombies as we speak.

I make my way back over to the tomb. Luckily, I still have the key. I literally let myself in, grab the purse and let myself quickly back out, not even knowing if grandma is still in there. And yes, I know you're dying to know...I did go back and get my Number Five. Also, Grandma was not, in fact, dead. Apparently, she had had a stroke and, last I heard, was being treated in a rehab facility nearby. Needless to say, her condo was taken off the market for the time being. Ugh, so close!

Even after this disastrous first outing, I kept plugging away. I felt like I was getting the hang of it. One time I took a well-to-do Venezuelan couple to look at one of those beautiful waterfront mansions I had envisioned. The listing agent met us there, and I have to say I felt somewhat intimidated. She was wearing a power suit and had thick black hair that I can only describe as coiffed. She looked amazing.

As we entered the living room, I was mesmerized by a wide expanse of windows overlooking the glistening waters of Tampa Bay. The well-coiffed listing agent began telling my clients about open water versus canals, and something about taxes and HOA fees and the difference between marble and granite. Suddenly, something caught my eye on the horizon. "Oh my God!" I squealed! "Look! Dolphins!" They all looked at me like I just threw up. "Dolphins," I repeated. My Venezuelan clients just looked at the listing agent longingly, wishing they could have her instead of me for their very own. From that time on during showings, I tried to act more professional, pretending I see dolphins and Italian marble every day.

One day my boss made me go sit at Starbucks and not come

back to the office until I had five names and phone numbers of people who might want to buy a house. I sat myself down in a corner and opened my laptop, knowing in my heart that there was no way I could do it. First of all, one guy in there was definitely homeless as he was wearing Crocs with the toes cut out and kept asking for free refills on water. Another table had what I think must have been a first date for an online match up as the woman was yammering away while twirling her hair and the man was staring at the door. Like I want any part of those two.

I stared at my computer screen and tried to think what I could do to look busy. I put my hands on the keys and I swear to you, before I knew what was happening, I was writing. I began writing about my divorce and it was not coming out bitchy and bitter. It was actually coming out sort of funny. I was cracking myself up over there in that little corner next to the FLORIDA mugs. I gave OW a fake name and she took shape on the page. That was the day my blog *Ex-Wife New Life* was born and it was truly a turning point in my life, although at that time I thought it was simply an outlet for my writing until the day I could return to college.

I really loved writing, but of course I knew it was not going to pay the bills. On the other hand, so far, between state fees, office fees, board fees and a new set of tires, real estate had only cost me several thousand dollars so, that was good. Still, I believed. I just knew any moment houses would start flying out the door, and I would be on easy street.

Chapter 6: It's a Mother of a Job

"Once you sign on to be a mother, that's the only shift they offer."—Jodi Picoult, My Sister's Keeper

Okay so, now I am a divorcee, a real estate agent specializing in finding one bedroom rentals for people with Great Danes and wild parrots—that's where the BIG money is—a blogger and a single mother of four kids ranging in age from fourteen to twenty-one. I realize that to really know me, you probably need to know them better, which will also give you insight as to why I have a prescription for a lifetime supply of an anti-depressant at my local pharmacy and why any time I see a phone call coming in from one of my kids, I answer the phone with, "What? What happened?"

My children came to me in perfect order: girl, boy, girl, boy. Frankly, I was so excited to see what they looked like I just couldn't stop myself from wanting more out of curiosity. *Ooooh...look at this one! She has blue eyes and dark hair! Let's have another one and see what that one looks like!* I carried Mackenzie, my first born, around like a mother cat, only putting her down when she fell asleep. Of course, she had a beautiful, fully decked out nursery, but slept in a bassinet next to our bed. Finally, after six months, Mark said enough was enough and moved her to her own room. She has never looked back. I, of course, have been in treatment ever since for irrational fear of a home invasion, but I guess we all have our stuff, right?

Two years after Mackenzie came my son James, another dark-haired blue-eyed wonder, tall and lanky like his dad and quite possibly the most sensitive of the four. Also, the most inquisitive. Once on their way to a baseball game, James turned to Mark and said, "Hey dad, where's the clitoris?" When Mark told me this story I, of course, said, "Well, I hope you were honest and told him you had no idea!" Why yes, my husband did leave me for another woman, why do you ask?

Being the most sensitive, James never handled change very well. In fact when he was in preschool in the two-year-old "grade" the teacher called me with a problem:

"We think James needs to go down a grade."

"Is there a grade lower than the two-year-old class?"

"Yes, the eighteen-month-old class."

"Well, what is it that he is behind in exactly?"

"Every time we switch activities, like go from coloring to play dough or from snack time to story hour, he cries. He does not like change."

Looking back, I now know that moving across the country when you are in eleventh grade and then watching your family come apart at the seams qualifies as change. I lost him for a while. One day he just got in his car and drove away instead of heading to his twelfth grade classes. I brought him home weeks later. He had fled to Kentucky and was living in his car in a friend's driveway. We both struggled through the pain, and although the road was long and painful, we traveled it together.

Then came Heather, a few years later and my first little blondie with eyes like a Furby. A beautiful child—wildly independent and afraid of nothing. I attribute this to our family vacation in Charleston when she was three. We had just toured the city and were heading out to a nearby island for a beach day. We were about ten minutes out when we realized we had left Heather sitting on the curb next to the horse drawn carriage we had just vacated. I think this may have left a mark.

Lastly came my Gabe, another blondie. Gabe looks like all the boys that never talked to me in middle school—tall, blonde and blue-eyed. He is now in college where he is doing quite well, but as a young child, I was often told, "Maybe he needs to be tested." One evening when he was roughly two years old, I was standing in front of the mirror putting on my face, which back then was a fifteen minute process as opposed to the full-length feature presentation that it is now. As I watched disbelievingly, Gabe picked up my eyelash curler, looked at it, then promptly clamped it down on his tongue, and began to scream. This was somewhat concerning.

Before we go any further, let me explain that the reason my children were not totally exemplary students and honor society members is that they were obviously too smart and they were bored in class. That is why sometimes they did not pay close attention to the teacher and may have missed out on a few important things, like math and science.

Anyway, as we settled into this new family dynamic, I began to notice that without Mark's large and looming presence, things were getting a little scary. It suddenly occurred to me that I was the only adult in the house. It's was sort of like that feeling I would get when my weird friend in high school spent the night, turned to me when my parents went out and said, "Hey, let's throw stuff out the window." Things could get away from me here...

Mark was and is a good father, paranoid about school buses—our kids were driven to school always—convinced there were pedophiles in any restroom his kids needed to use, and great with school projects. He once built an entire Roman house out of sugar cubes. He participated in a lot of their activities, although he often embarrassed the kids with somewhat inappropriate humor. One time when he was coaching little league he asked, "Okay, who here thinks they would like to try pitching?" One little, rather uncoordinated kid, stood up and Mark replied, "You can't even walk kid, sit down." Another time he was on a school rafting trip with Mackenzie's eighth grade class. He asked the young teacher in charge if he would like to share his lunch. When Mr. Wittle replied his girlfriend had packed his lunch for him, Mark looked around at the kids and said, "Oh, which one is she?"

Now with him no longer present in the house, I began to notice weird things...like a kitten living in Heather's room, screens mysteriously off the windows in Gabe's room and a homemade fire pit in the back yard with the charred remains of a plastic dinner plate and a Red Bull can. To make matters worse, during my first holiday season alone, I received an e-mail from Mark saying that he would be out of town for New Year's. To me, out of town means a day at the Gap Outlet, which is about an hour from my house. To him it means a week in Switzerland skiing the Alps. By the way, he skis? Who knew?

Instantly, fear set in. I mean, we are talking New Year's Eve with three teenagers at home. Suddenly, I had the intense desire to call Mark and invite him back. "Sure, you can bring OW, the more the merrier." I mean seriously, what is a little adultery? It's not like he tried to kill me or anything, like the husbands on Dateline who think no one will notice their wife is missing and then look totally shocked when she is found in little pieces in the front yard, like, "Oh my gosh, how did THAT get there?" They can have the master, I will bunk in with Heather, and OW and I can share the household chores, though word has it she is a neat-freak, so I hope she doesn't look in the pantry, where there are piles of opened Oreo sleeves each containing half of a cookie.

The fear only intensified when I went searching in my daughter's bathroom cabinet for her hair straightener during the last week of that December. I had decided to try a new sleek look that looked great on Rhianna and reinvent myself for the new year. Unfortunately, this did not turn out well for me. I ended up with a few singed wisps across my forehead and a big red burn across my left ear. Still, not only did I find the straightener, but I also came across a small metal barrel with the word VODKUH written across the front with a Sharpie. Two things became instantly clear, 1. Some shit was about to go down and 2. Private school is a huge rip off.

This culminated in a New Year's party at my house where I went around smelling everyone's breath and making sure the only 'high" the kids were enjoying was a sugar high from Orange Crush.

One night, a few months later, just as I had fallen asleep, there was a knock on the door. Standing there were two police officers. First thought? This cannot be good. Second thought? I hope my boobs are not hanging out from under my T-shirt. Turns out they were simply inquiring if James, then eighteen, had made it home safely. Would I mind checking? I knew he'd come in because he had a curfew of midnight and I heard him rustling around preparing his favorite snack of potato chips and ranch dressing at about that time. Still, I thought, "Now this is why I live in a gated community. Everyone keeping an eye out for each other." I peeked in and saw my darling boy, fast asleep, safe and sound. I reported back to the officers, "Yes, he's here, sound asleep. Thanks for checking. Goodnight!" They then asked if I would mind stepping outside to inspect his vehicle. Oh, crap. Whenever a cop uses the word *vehicle*, you know you are fucked.

"We think your son may have been involved in an accident involving property damage." I started to argue that there is no way that sleeping boy in there could have done anything like that, when I noticed black tire tracks coming from the gate leading into my driveway, where my son's car sat with two flat front tires and a piece of concrete stuck to his bumper. If one considers running into a steel lamppost property damage, then, yes, it looks as if their hunch was correct. Luckily for us, in the end, it resultedin a hefty fine...and payment for the damage... Needless to say, this resulted in a loss of driving privileges for James and blissful nights of sound sleep for me.

Of course, I had to ask, "Just wondering. Did you think I wouldn't notice this or what?

"No, I was gonna tell you in the morning and then tell the security guy that we would pay for it."

"What happened? How did you hit a huge steel pole that does not move?"

"I was swerving not to hit a deer. You know Mom, I'd freak if I hit a deer."

And because I, too, am an animal lover, it totally made sense.

On an up note, socially, my kids seemed to be really thriving. Suddenly, our house was the place to be. It made me feel great my kids had so many friends. Most weekend nights, a group of kids would arrive at our home and head out to the garage. Now that our three-car garage had only one car in it, it was a great gathering place for them, and Heather, then fifteen, had arranged a circle of chairs so that her friends could sit, laugh and share stories with each other. I did my part by keeping the garage fridge stocked with sodas and popsicles and assumed they were enjoying rousing games of Twister.

One evening, my dear friends Stacy and Ken came by for an impromptu dinner of pasta with tomatoes and anchovies. They were the only married friends I could stand to be around because they were always fighting. Stacy and I met when our parents were on the same bowling league at Ten Pins Lanes in St. Petersburg. She was five. I was eight. And, yes, our moms had their own balls and carrying bags.

Here's the thing about Stacy: I love her. She is my bestie; however, she is one of those people who can't understand when someone royally fucks up. She *never* does. Sometimes it's hard being best friends with her because she's one of those types who succeeds at everything, then keeps it to herself. She graduated law school at the top of her class, but most people don't know that because she doesn't talk about it. I, on the other hand, pretty much tell everyone I've met that in third grade my story, "Life Under the Sea," was published in the school newspaper.

Anyway, here's how Stacy's divorce would go if it ever happened:

After representing herself in her own divorce, she would walk away with lifetime alimony plus a brand new car of her choice delivered to her driveway every year.

She would become famous for the excellent deal she brokered for herself and then be sought out by Gwyneth Paltrow to represent her when she finally realizes that Chris is not coming back to her and Apple and Moses.

On her flight out to California to consult with GP, she meets a man in first class, who happens to be a mega Hollywood producer that falls madly in love with her. He flies her out to Beverly Hills every other weekend when her ex has the kids, and eventually dies in a paragliding accident, leaving her his entire estate.

She writes a book about her experiences that becomes a mega movie and gets to meet Meryl Streep, thereby, living out my dream.

Anyway, I handed each of them a glass of wine and Ken asked where the kids were. I told him out in the garage playing with friends.

"Okay, I want to go say hi to those guys," he said.

Stacy and I continued chopping garlic and sipping on Chianti when I happened to notice Ken had been gone for over thirty minutes. About that time, the door to the garage opened and Ken entered the kitchen, his eyes glazed over and a very stupid grin on his face. Instantly, I knew something not good was going on out there. Definitely, not good.

"Oh my God, "he breathed. "There's a whole world out there."

Right about that time, I heard the main garage door open and the sound of numerous cars starting up and roaring out of the driveway.

"What are you talking about?" I asked him.

"Come with me," he slurred.

In the now empty garage, he opened what I thought was a small storage closet, that had contained two paint cans and extra bricks for the driveway pavers, but now appeared to be Bob Marley's living room, may he rest in peace. For starters, there was an orange Peace poster and a pink feather boa strung up along the wall. Strands of multicolored beads hung from the ceiling to the floor. There were strewn pillows on the floor, and several ashtrays that held burning cigarettes, along with other still lit smokeable things. On the back of the door was a hand written sign that said NARNIA. This, at least, had been spelled correctly. A boom box was playing *Don't Worry Be Happy* and the whole garage smelled like dead skunks.

Oh my God, dudes. You are so busted.

Immediately, I headed to Heather's room and banged on the door.

"Oh my god!" I screamed. "What are you thinking?"

"Calm down, Mom. It's no big deal. We weren't even doing anything. God!"

I immediately went back to the scene of the crime and ripped everything from the walls. I threw it all into the outside trash cans. I doused the ashtrays with water and dumped them into a trash bag the size of an army tank. I folded up all the chairs, both in the storage closet and the others that looked like they were set for a kindergarten story hour. I then went inside and waited for the DEA helicopter to land on my roof. Stacy and Ken sat at the kitchen table, slurping up pasta.

"Kids," Ken said. "What are ya gonna do?"

"Live the rest of my life with a cell mate who calls me Princess," I answered.

Okay, yes, the light went on. I realized I needed to toughen up and pay attention. This would take more than the month-long grounding I had just put in place to iron out. My kids were on a collision course to disaster, and I needed to reel them in and set them straight.

Yes, this was a major fuck up, but I have to say, though they may have made a few bad decisions from time to time that may have resulted in some legal ramifications now and then, there was one thing they did not do that I will always be grateful for: they never used their father's new love against me to get their way. If I said no to something they wanted or punished them for something that was totally not their fault, they never said, "Well, OW likes when our friends come over and smoke on the patio," or "OW never cares if we sneak friends in through the pool bathroom door," or "How come you have a haircut like a man?"

In fact, they always let me know I was their mother and there would be no replacement. When they'd come home from a visit with their dad and OW, I would casually ask them "What did you have for dinner?"

"OW made steak," they reported, "but yours is way better."

Finally, they did let one thing slip and I pounced on it. It had come to my attention that for the holidays OW made homemade pretzels. Now, I know we're supposed to be archenemies.

She stole my husband, blah, blah, but homemade pretzels? I asked my oldest daughter, Mackenzie, "Homemade pretzels? How are they?"

"Seriously Mom, they are so good," she replied, then caught herself, "I mean if you even like pretzels, that is."

Please. I love dough. I love salt. I love pretzels! A deal was brokered. Through anonymous channels, a piece of my homemade chocolate cheesecake was smuggled to Mark and two homemade pretzels were then delivered into my hungry little hands. Yes, they were delicious. Maybe not worth leaving your wife over, but really, really good. Stop judging. If you can't beat 'em...

Other perks followed. Turns out, she is one of those holiday freaks. She even has one of those Halloween sweaters with an embroidered pumpkin on the front and dresses up to hand out the candy. I, on the other hand, stick a bowl of last year's sale candy on the stoop with a sticky note that says "HELP YOURSELF. DO NOT RING BELL." For Valentine's Day, each kid came home with a box of expensive chocolates and then she gave them huge Easter baskets. I told them to be sure to ask for extra chocolate malted milk ball eggs. Also, skip the jellybeans. Gross.

One afternoon Heather came home from school with a sewing project of which we were both clueless. She mentioned that OW had a sewing machine. I dropped her off at Daddy's with a bag of fabric and a spool of thread. She returned home with an award winning quilt square with her name sewed into the binding with glittery thread. Sewed in! That certainly helped our grade average in the class the school calls Life Skills, but what I call, "I Don't Really Want to go to College Anyway, so Where Can I Hang Out Until the Bell Rings?" Sweeeeet.

Before I knew it, a year had passed. Mackenzie was living in New York City and had just taken her first job with a teensy tiny, itty bitty, PR firm, with a teensy tiny salary to match. I knew that Mark was helping her out, and I suggested that perhaps she try to find a job that could at least cover her bills. She certainly put me in my place when she declared, "Mom, other than my rent, electricity and food, I am totally supporting myself."

Anyway, about a month after she started, she called me with some startling news:

"Hi, Mac, how's it going in the city today?"

"Not good."

"Oh no, what's wrong, sis?"

"I'm being sued by Leonardo DiCaprio."

"Ummm, what? Leonardo DiCaprio of *Titanic* is suing you?"

"Yes, Mom. That's what I said."

"But Mackenzie, why?"

"Well, I was in a club, and he was in the same club at some private thing, and I sort of reported what I overheard him saying in return for someone plugging one of my clients in the same paper. And he is super pissed."

"Oh my God! You were in a club with Leonardo DiCaprio? How does he look?"

"Mom! This is serious. I'm going to have to hire a lawyer and it might be real expensive. I mean, this could be huge."

I think that by, "I am going to have to hire a lawyer" she means, *you* are going to have to hire a lawyer and by "huge" she means I may have to sell my wedding ring to cover this disaster. Now, let's look at my financial status, as of right now. On top of giving up Boar's Head for Oscar Meyer and buying generic shampoo from Walgreen's that makes my hair so flat I look like a wet ferret, I will now be writing a check to Leonardo DeCaprio? Will he be coming in his private jet to pick it up, or do I just overnight it? Wouldn't it be cheaper to just have it automatically deposited in his account? Ugh!! If I could just talk to him, maybe I could make him see this is all a misunderstanding and really, no one cares that much that he said, "Everybody wants to be me," as Mackenzie reported. And so what? I for one would love to be you, Leonardo.

Listen Leo, if someone ever said they wanted to be me, I would freaking tweet it all over the place. I would have it as the new cover photo on my Facebook page. I would actually pay somebody to say it. So, let's just chalk this up to a little free publicity for you and another reason I wish Mackenzie had gone to nursing school, and call it a day.

In the end, Mackenzie's kind boss paid what luckily turned out to be a nominal legal fee, a retraction was printed, and Leonardo went on to weather the crisis by starring in the remake of *The Great Gatsby,* and thankfully, was able to get his life back on track.

We were trying to do the same thing, and, basically, we were succeeding. Mark and OW had recently bought a golden retriever puppy, so I nixed the idea of having them move in. I dug deep and began to take charge of the household. Screens were reinstalled, the fire pit was disassembled and, as for the kitten that had taken up residence in Heather's room, Jet is now the center of my life giving me plenty to talk about at parties and making me one of the most fascinating people in the room. Enough said there.

Curfews were put in place and enforced, and a sense of order began to prevail. This is not to say that they didn't try to pull one over on me occasionally. I mean, they still sort of knew that if they could get me in front of a *Real Housewives* marathon at night, I was pretty much oblivious to the world around me. Gabe tried this approach and almost pulled it off.

One night I went down to his room to say goodnight. I knocked loudly and waited for permission to enter as, without going into too much detail, every mother knows that entering a teenage boy's room without prior permission could result in a very embarrassing situation for her and years of therapy for him. Don't do it. After several knocks and no answer, I assumed he was asleep and, for some reason, perhaps I had just watched *Kramer vs. Kramer* for the fifty-millionth time, I had a strong urge to check in on him. By now you know my obsession with Meryl, my heart was swelling with that "my children are so precious" feeling. So I peeked my head in to see his sweet sleeping face and instantly I could tell something was wrong. There was a shape in the bed, and pillows were plumped up and folded over, but unless he had turned into the Elephant Man in the last two hours, there was no way there was a human under there. Further inspection revealed three rolled up hoodies and a heart shaped pillow that his girlfriend had given him, covered with a blanket where his precious head should have been.

Several things were at play here: 1. My son lied to me and told me he was going to sleep 2. My son had probably spent more time assembling a fake human form under blankets than he had spent on his tenth grade science project, where he dropped an egg from a window and timed how long it took for it to hit my pool deck, and 3. It is eleven o'clock on a Sunday night and my child isn't at home. These are all very upsetting events. However, even more upsetting is the fact that even if I had fallen for it and assumed that the disfigured mass under the blankets was my son, it still wouldn't explain why his car was gone. Maybe he does need to be tested.

I immediately called his girlfriend's house, where he was rustled out and home within thirty minutes. Good try. Sheer brilliance.

Despite these occasional setbacks, I was really doing it. I was a divorced mom raising kids. Yes, their dad was nearby when not swooshing down Swiss mountains, but I was the one who dealt with the day-to-day ups, downs, disappearances, and threats from Oscar-nominated actors. We were all, in a way, growing up.

Like most divorced parents, I'll always carry a lot of guilt. Most of us feel guilty that we just couldn't hold it together, couldn't make a go of if even "for the sake of the children." My children have seen me at my very worst, at times a screaming, crying, wandering ball of snot. At other times, a zombie vampire, sleeping all day and only coming out at night to eat dry cereal out of a box and return to bed In my defense, I plan to spend the rest of my life trying to make it up to them, even if it means buying them all Porsches once my movie comes out. Ironically, I'm thinking of asking Leonardo to play Mark.

A few months back, I was in New York City visiting my sister. We were sitting around her apartment and Laurie, a good friend of hers, had stopped by with bagels and lox. In between bites, I was filling her in on my life as it is now.

"Do you talk to Mark much?"

"No not much, mainly about the kids. We had a good laugh last week about something Gabe did."

"I don't know how you can talk to him, much less have a good laugh. How can you not just absolutely hate him?"

Right at that time there was a knock on the door. Victoria opened it and there stood my beautiful Mackenzie, drinking a Starbucks, her dark hair pulled into a tight pony tail and her long legs wrapped in black exercise tights.

As Mackenzie ran over and gave me a big hug, I looked at Laurie.

"That's how," I answered.

Chapter 7: Love Long Walks on the Beach

"How many of you ever started dating because you were too lazy to commit suicide?"—Judy Tenuta

I'm ashamed to admit that when I realize I was soon to be divorced, my first thought was remarriage. If I could just slide another man into Mark's vacant position, I'd probably be okay. This, of course, was based totally on fear. I've had a husband since before I was legally of drinking age. I could see definite problems on the horizon. For instance, what do I tell the mechanic at Toyota, the cable guy trying to get me to upgrade our HBO package, and the lady at the bank calling me to offer us a sweet refinancing deal on our mortgage? Do I say, "I'll have to check with my husband first? If I have no husband, then I am no wife and that makes me...what? Who?

Later, when I was in the thick of divorce, I entered my man-hating phase. During this time, if you'd been introduced to me at a party or a school luncheon or were in front of me at the checkout line in Publix, I was likely to start a conversation with, "Hi, aren't men the worst?" and then you might say, "Hoo boy! I hear ya, can't wait for football season to end," and then I would glare at you, start crying and say, "No really, aren't they?" at which time, you'd pretend you forgot they had a sale on fire-roasted canned tomatoes and calmly back out of line.

Now that my divorce decree is firmly adhered to a page in my scrapbook, my children are in a good place, meaning there are currently no legal proceedings filed against them and our garage marijuana dispensary is closed down, I sort of started to miss the company of a man. I missed hearing a deep rumbling voice, I missed hairy arms—mine don't count—I missed bed talking, you know when you lie in bed just shooting the breeze. This may sound weird, but I even missed waking up in the morning and walking into a bathroom with the smell of shaving cream and after shave wafting around me, that wet, steamy fog that says a man is starting his day. I used to love watching Mark shave, leaning into the mirror with a towel around his waist. I'd sit on the edge of the tub, admiring the way he stretched his mouth one way and then the other, deftly maneuvering a razor around his face. It's such a *man* thing.

Between you and me, another weird sort of thing was happening, too. I was starting to get a little tingling now and then, you know...down there. I might be watching a movie or see a picture of Brad Pitt in *People Magazine,* or even hearing a man's deep laugh over the din of conversation in a restaurant, and I would get this weird feeling. At first I was like, I hope I'm not getting another yeast infection, and then I realized what was happening. I missed a *penis*. That's right, I said it...I missed having sex!

Let me explain to you why this is a scary thought. I realized that in order to have sex, I was probably going to have to take my clothes off and no one had seen my naked body in the last thirty years except myself, Mark, my gynecologist, and my cleaning lady, who one time had walked into the bathroom without knocking and then ran out yelling, "Oh *dios mio*!" as I stepped out of the shower. You can see my reason for concern.

I had lost quite a bit of weight while on the Divorce Diet and for all intents and purposes, my body looked pretty good. I don't want to paint myself as an overweight woman camped out all day in front of the television with a bag of cheese puffs, like a family member from *Honey Boo Boo*. Though divorce had ravaged my heart and soul, it had been pretty good to my body. Still there were scars that told my story, including my tubal ligation scar that I got from the procedure I told the doctor I wanted, seconds after Gabe's birth, with tears running down my face.

"You don't have to do it, I'll get a vasectomy," Mark said as they wheeled me into a nearby operating room.

"No you won't," I said, with a sob.

There was the scar from my ovary removal and there was the freckle on my butt that Mark always touched whenever my ass was exposed. The thought of another man seeing these atrocities was almost unthinkable. I mean, isn't this the nightmare that we've all had, the one where we show up naked to a public event—in this case a make-out session in a strange man's bedroom—and everybody points and laughs? I truly wanted to believe that another man could accept and even learn to love these imperfections.

The next major hurdle I had to cross was feet. I have this thing about feet and the thought of some man in my bed with gross scaly feet or those sick yellow toenails made me gag. I must admit, I was a bit spoiled in this regard. I mean Mark had very nice feet and kept them nicely groomed. In fact, his were smoother than mine and he often referred to my toenails as talons, after I had sliced his leg open a few times while watching TV in bed.

Assuming I could overcome these obstacles, where was I going to meet a man? The only single man I knew was Frankie, our handyman, and he wore his T-shirts like Brittney Spears in the nineties and smelled like cheese. I could only imagine his feet. My friends couldn't help me. They were all married as were *their* friends. Also, I noticed they were keeping really tight reins on their husbands whenever I was around; like if we were all at a dinner party and I was speaking to Ted Rosengarten, suddenly Marcy would appear and be all, "Honey you have to come over here and try this guac," leading him away by the arm.

Here's the thing about that. Somehow these ladies must have forgotten that they've shared with me over the years, things about their husbands that were not only deeply personal but sort of gross. For instance, I knew that Ted Rosengarten spit when he kissed and that Marcy had to constantly wipe her mouth on her pillow during sex. I knew that Phil Lerner clipped his toenails in bed and that his wife Stacy nearly gagged when she heard the clip-clip-clip of the tail trimmers. I knew that Mark Chapman watched fat lady porn on his tablet when he thought

Lisa was sleeping. So ladies, please, fear not. I have no intention of dating one of your hubbies.

Luckily, through my hours of late night TV viewing, I had learned a lot about YourLoveConnection and I really trusted that old guy who apparently accompanies everyone on their dates, even though he was super creepy. I thought I would give it a try.

I logged onto the site and began to fill out the questionnaire, which was like five hundred pages long but promises that, "It is the first step towards finding the love of your life." Okay, I'm down with that.

Two hours later, I was only half way done and realized that *I* don't want to date *me*. I was so bored. This was way too much information for some poor shlub to take in. For instance, "Your date takes you to a rockin' party where there's not one familiar face, what do you do?"

a. Stick to him or her like glue
b. Head to the bar and let him/her enjoy the party
c. Totally kill it by introducing yourself and making friends
d. Beg off and watch Netflix alone

My answer: Grab a glass of chardonnay and head to the bathroom where I would call my sister while looking at my pores through their awesome magnifying mirror.

OR

In 15 years you will be:
a. Slick urban apartment
b. Cute little cottage in a quaint town
c. Safely tucked away in a suburban community
d. Country manor

My answer: Parents spare bedroom with a cat named Mr. Whiskers.

No, this wasn't going to work for me, but I wasn't ready to give up yet. I decided to try another site that perhaps was a bit more user friendly. Game Set Match.com had a pretty good reputation, so I went that route and after answering a few routine questions realized the hard part was just beginning because next I would need photos. I began to peruse my photo library from the last two years. Let's see, here I am after taking sailing lessons, Mark's suggestion for something fun we could do together, wearing a ball cap, long shorts, white boating non-skid shoes and a fanny pack, with a look on my face that says, "Couldn't we do ballroom dancing or wine tasting?" Side note, months later, after some intense FaceBook stalking, I found a picture of OW at the helm of a sail boat wearing a white sundress, barefoot with her long blonde hair back in a ponytail. I guess Swiss people don't believe in reliable deck shoes to avoid slipping.

Here's one of me in the driver's seat of a Home Depot delivery truck, which I rented to bring home a new gas grill. I remember sitting at a stop light when one of my old tennis partners pulled up a long side me and gave me the thumbs up, then texted me, "Congrats on your new job! You go girl!"

There was one of Mark and me at a seafood restaurant. I, of course, am wearing a lobster bib. Ugh. Finally, I found one that had been taken when the wind hit me just right, covering that slight bald spot I have on the right side of my head, which I still say was from my mother making my pony tails too tight. I was up and running.

I sent my new single self out into the Internet universe, hoping it landed on a normal guy's computer and not on some serial killer's or sick pervert looking for his next sex slave/laundress.

The next morning my inbox was flooded with winks, flirts and messages. Oh my God, I thought, it would take me months to have sex with all these awesome, handsome, eligible, age appropriate, totally single men.

Here are just a few that stood out:

"Hey pritty ladie"—standing with shirt off, gut out holding big dead fish.

"Let's make some music"—looked like Yoda.

"I know I am younger than your desired age range, but will you dominate me?" —thirty-four and, unfortunately, very cute.

"Would love to meet in person, I will contact you, DO NOT CONTACT ME!"—George Segal-ish looking.

Then finally…

"Hi, I live in your area and think it would be great to meet up." —Looked like Ben Stiller, his screen name JewishDoc1665.

Folks, we have a winnah!

Please, it's a no brainer. I, Jewish woman, will go out with him, Jewish doctor. Already, I'm planning our wedding, which will be held in the Temple Beth-El, near my parent's home in Sarasota. He and my mom will bond as he replaces her at home blood pressure machine with the real thing. I guess me and the kids will just move into his place, or wait, no, he will probably want to buy us our own new place, maybe near the hospital, so he can run home for quick romantic lunches and hot steamy sex on our king-sized bed covered with a fluffy white down comforter from the Macy's Hotel collection.

We began to e-mail back and forth and I found out more about him. Mainly, he lived and practiced in the nearby area and that he was, in fact, a chiropractor. Shut up! It still counts!

After a few days of this, JewishDoc suggested a meeting at a local establishment, which he described as a really nice restaurant on the water. We set a date and time, and, just like that, I was back out there.

Instantly, fear set in. I mean, the last time I was on a date I was wearing Bonnie Belle Cotton Candy lip smackers and Buffalo sandals. What does one do to prepare for a date these days? Once again I turned to Google for answers. Typing in "Preparing for a date," I thought I would find cool make-up techniques, trendy clothing looks, and even interesting ways to start a conversation. Instead, one of the first articles I came across was, "Tips for Anal Bleaching." Huh? What the fuck is this now?

Here's the thing: I know I have one, but I have really never looked at it and have no interest in us introducing ourselves at this point. The article says, "Anal bleaching allows both men and women to look their best, especially in their most intimate areas." Let me get this straight, on top of worrying about waxing my mustache and eyebrows and viciously ripping the hair of off my vagina, I now have to worry about the color of my anus? Is this a joke? I want to look my absolute best for my first face-to-face meeting with my online date/fiancé, but I'm drawing the line here.

Anyway, I decided to take the more conventional route of a new outfit and lipstick. At this point, I was totally into my Anthropologie phase where I was buying lots of long flowy tops, coffee mugs with peacocks on them and big letter A's covered in fabric. I sashayed myself in there and picked out a beautiful red shawl—this was during the brief shawl resurgence before everyone realized that we all looked like that weird librarian in junior high—to wear with cool jeans and a peasant blouse. Don't need to say it, I know.

Early in the day of my big debut as a single woman on a date, I called Stacy, "Please come over and see what I'm wearing. Be honest."

She showed up an hour later with her five year old twins, A and A. I gave them each a can of ginger ale and put them in front of the Wii. I needed all of Stacy's attention.

I put on my hip, cool but sophisticated, glamorous yet understated, trendy but classic date outfit and expected Stacy's eyes to light up with a mixture of awe and envy.

"What is with you and the peasant blouses?"

"I think it' s a really good look for me," I explained.

"I think it's a really good look for you if you are hanging laundry in a shtetl in World War II Poland, but not sure if it's great for date night."

I called Mackenzie. She was the only one of my kids I felt could handle the thought of their mother on a date.

"What are you wearing?" she asked.

"I have super cool jeans, a peas—, um, a nice top, laced up espadrilles and a red shawl."

"Mom! A shawl? Who wears a shawl? Who even says the word shawl?!!"

"Mackenzie. That's what we are wearing in Florida. It's all the rage."

"Oh. Well sounds really nice. Have fun!"

Can I tell you the emotions that ran through me as I drove to the designated date location? Excitement, anxiety and sadness.

When I stopped to think about it, the last time I had been on a date as a single woman was with Mark, and we all know how that turned out. Such hopes. Such promise. Such good times ahead. I knew there would never be another man who would know me the way Mark did, who would be able to picture me at sixteen walking down a high school hallway. No other man would be dropping me off at my job at a vet's office, God willing, on his way to his college classes, or holding my hand during Lamaze class. So many life-changing moments, yet so much unspeakable pain. Was I really ready to face the possibility of another failed marriage, even if it was with a doctor? Okay, chiropractor!

On the other hand, the thought of going through life with no male companionship didn't sound good either. One evening soon after my divorce was final, I was getting dressed to go out for a girl's night, when I reached around to zip the top of my dress. It was not easy. Suddenly, I realized I would be zipping up my own dress for the rest of my life. I dissolved into tears as I sat down on the side of my bed. I can't tell you how sad it made me. Sure, I missed sex, but I also missed the little intimacies—the dress zipping, the tie straightening; the pulling up the hair from underneath collar in the back. That would be his, not mine, my stylist actually used clippers on my neck line. I wanted help with my zipper. I realized I was going to have to dive in and learn to doggy paddle across the pool. Again.

When I arrived at our date location, I parked my car in the gravel lot and tried to avoid getting little pebbles between my toes in my new espadrilles. Now, JewishDoc1665 had described this as *a really nice restaurant on the water*. I would sum it up more as a broken down Tiki hut on a trash-ridden canal. I had pictured us sharing intimate conversation over Tuna Tartar and dirty martinis, but okay, I guess gator bites and beer is fine, too.

I approached the two hostesses/meth heads and said,

"Hi, I'm meeting a date here," and they were like, "Well, good for you. So?"

So then I said, "Is there anyone here waiting for me?" and they said, without looking up,

"Don't see anyone," and so I said,

"Can I just take a look around the bar?" and they said, "Whatever," so I began to walk around the bar in my red shawl, trying to look like I belonged there, when in fact I felt more like Princess Di visiting a leper colony. I slowly made my way around the bar looking for a Jewish chiropractor. One guy looked up at me from beneath his baseball cap and said, "Huh?" which I took to mean, "Why are you wearing a shawl at a Tiki bar?"

I made one complete loop around and decided perhaps JewishDoc1665 had to do a last minute back adjustment and was just running a little late. Once again, I approached the hostesses/meth heads and said, "Hi, my date is running a little late, is it okay if I just sit here?" pointing to a little stool next to the hostess stand, and one of them said, "We ain't supposed to let anyone sit there," so I had to continue to stand there like a moron as I let it sink in, that, in fact, my date/fiancé was not coming, especially after I sent the text, "Hi! I'm here!" and heard nothing back.

Finally, I made my way back to the parking lot, not even caring if there were pebbles in my espadrilles. As I opened my car door one of the meth heads yelled, "I like your shawl!!" so the night was not a total loss.

I drove straight to Stacy's house, where her husband Ken opened the door for me.

"I can't even give this shit away," I said. I then proceeded to drink a bottle of pinot noir at their kitchen table and, later, backed my car up into their tree. I then drove home—never, never do this— and went to bed, only to wake up in the middle of the night, remember that weird bump I felt when I backed up my car in their yard and texted Stacy to make sure A and A were both in their beds.

Don't worry. They were.

Okay, I agree. Not a great start to finding male companionship. But no. I did not give up! I licked my wounds for a few days, which included a lot of phone calls back and forth between my sister and me.

"Do you think he saw me in the parking lot wearing that stupid shawl and just left?"

"No, I think he's an asshole."

"Do you think he saw me and thought I was old?"

"Uh, no, I think he's an asshole."

"Oh. So, I just read there is a new grilled cheese food truck in New York. Have you seen it?"

"No, but I will definitely be on the lookout."

Anyway, back to the drawing board. I had had a flirt message from a guy named Chad. Chad liked me because I had filled in my weight on the profile. He had been on dates where the woman showed up and was fat, which he said, "She obviously neglected to tell me," and, in his eyes, that gave him the absolute right to get up and leave, if he was lucky enough to see her before she saw him.

Once we got it out of the way that I was not currently obese, we began firing those flirty e-mails back and forth, which I think is the best part of online dating. You can be whoever you want in those e-mails.

HIM "I like a girl who's honest about her weight. Are you being honest?"

ME: "I'm honest and then some."

HIM: "Okay, what do you honestly think of me so far?"

ME: "I think you have great eyes and a fat phobia. Honest."

You get the idea. I wanted to portray myself as a concoction of Chelsea Handler and Lauren Bacall in *To Have and Have Not,* when she tells Humphrey Bogart, "You just put your lips together and blow..." Cool, hip, sexy and funny, letting him picture me lying in bed drinking a glass of Malbec and typing away on my laptop.

In fact, on this particular day, I was sitting in my kitchen with a pot of macaroni and cheese waiting for Gabe to get home from school, who was at least thirty minutes over due. Finally, I heard his big feet ambling up to the front door.

Slamming the computer shut I said, "Gabe. Where have you been? Why are you so late?"

"Oh, sorry Mom. Our bus driver likes to drive us past his

old house every day. He got divorced and lives with his mom now."

"Oh God. Maybe I'll start picking you up again after school. No wonder Daddy never let you ride the bus."

"No way! He gives us gum."

Sometimes, especially after an exchange such as this with one of my children, it almost seemed as though I was two separate people. One of me was, above all, a mother trying to keep four kids on the straight and narrow, providing love and a new found stability to their precious lives. The other me was a single woman hoping to find love/long term relationship/Jewish wedding/Sunday night dinners, where man cooks up fabulous meals for my parents and children, while telling funny stories about all the cute things I did that week. First, of course, I had to have a date with a man who actually went on the date WITH me.

I began to realize I needed to do a little compartmentalizing of my life. The mother who was listening to Heather tell me why her Art teacher hates her could not be the same person who ran into her room to check the computer every time her e-mail dinged. I made a conscious decision to be mother by day and sultry vixen single woman in demand by eligible, age-appropriate men with good hair by night. In other words, I only logged on to my Game Set Match.com account in the evenings and on weekends, and maybe from my phone when I was sitting in a cubicle at my real estate office pretending to be engaged in conversation with a potential buyer every time my boss walked by.

"What is your price range? Mmmmhhhmm. And when were you hoping to relocate? Oh? Not for another year? Okay. I'll check back."

Anyway, back to Chad.

Chad worked in the IT department of a big computer firm here in town. Smart. I like it. It was about a week after our e-mails began flying that we took it a step further. We scheduled a phone call. Now just let me say here that I don't like talking on the phone, unless it's to Stacy or my sister and in that case I probably am not only talking on the phone, I may also be peeing, eating cereal, brushing my teeth or even plucking a stray mustache hair. I especially hate when I'm talking to someone by cellphone and everything I say repeats itself a second later, making me think there's either a man or a woman with a very deep voice in the room and I'm on speaker and they are all laughing at me. With online dating though, it's a necessary evil. So here's how it happened.

"So, do you think we're ready for a phone call?"

"Already? What kind of girl do you think I am?

"A thin one who can talk, I hope."

"Well, alright. I guess we are ready to take the next step."

"Okay, I'll send my number. Call me tonight at seven."

"Nope. I don't call men. I'll send my number and you call me at nine."

And here I have to tell you that I really don't call men because back in my teens, my mom told me if I called a boy it looked desperate and slutty. I know it's ridiculous in this day and age, but I tell my daughters that, too. I think living with the fear of looking like a desperate slut may be one of the curses of being a Jewish woman along with needing our mother's approval when we pick out a new couch and thinking we have diabetes whenever we're thirsty. Forget about the fact that by giving out my number I'm opening myself up to sickos and rapists who will do that reverse cellphone look-up thing and be waiting by the curb with a machete and a heavy-duty trash bag when I drag my garbage can out on Tuesday mornings. Above all, I must not appear slutty.

The phone call went down and, to be honest, I don't remember it word for word. I remember there was a lot of giggling, and we set a dinner date for the following weekend. I do remember telling him about my first date debacle and he promised me he would be there. We were all set for Mitchell's Seafood Restaurant at the Westshore Plaza on Saturday.

For this date, I chose the same outfit as before, minus the shawl. Don't ask me why. I just couldn't give up on that peasant blouse. I'm telling you, it's a good look for me. My jeans and espadrilles once again completed the ensemble. I felt ready.

I arrived at Mitchell's Seafood and entered the bar. It was

packed! I didn't see Chad. He swore to me his picture was very recent, and I couldn't just stand there like an idiot, so I ordered a glass of wine. It occurred to me that I had never been in a bar by myself. I tried to remember what Mark used to do. Did he pay the bill or wait until we were at to our table? What if I waited and then Chad thought I expected him to pay for it? Should he pay for it? Was it more than twenty dollars? Because that's all I had on me. Ugh. Being single was getting harder by the minute.

I just went ahead and gave the bartender the twenty, left five on the counter, and took five for my purse. I'd just taken a big gulp of my Kendall Jackson chardonnay when I suddenly felt a hand on my back and turned to look at the face that it belonged to. Chad.

"Hi," he said, giving me a hug. "Were you getting nervous?"

"Not at all," I said. "There's plenty of men here to choose from."

Oh my God! Why did I say that? Slut! Slut! Slut!

Chad had thought ahead and made a reservation, so the hostess guided us right over to a table. We sat down and began making small talk.

"So, do I look like my picture?"

"Yeah, you do," I answered. "Do I?"

"Yes, happily you do."

Chad did look exactly like his photo. He was a compact guy, about five-foot ten, which was the shortest I would go and said so in my profile, with a crew cut and wire rimmed glasses. He had a nice build and through his khakis I could see the outlines of his leg muscles that I knew must be really strong from his daily tennis games. He wore nice slip on loafers and a navy blue polo shirt, tucked in, with a belt. I tried to imagine his feet, but I really wasn't ready to go there yet.

Still, things were off to a great start and I have to tell you, chills went up my spine when I felt that hand on my back. I glanced at his hands several times during dinner and imagined them wandering around various parts of my body. Tingle. Tingle. Tingle. This could be it! I could see him and my dad sitting around talking about the differences between Dell and Mac computers. Maybe he could get Gabe interested in taking up tennis and they would spend Saturday mornings together playing on a doubles team. It's all falling into place.

We began to peruse the menu and that's when something very strange happened. I began to get overwhelmingly sad. It started when I began to look over the appetizers and instantly picked out what I know Mark would have ordered—the fried calamari and from the salads, the Blue cheese Wedge, and for his entree, crab legs. Thus my monthly trip to CVS for his cholesterol meds. Oh no, were my eyes actually tearing up? I began chanting to myself, *Do-not-cry-in-front-of-Chad! Do-not-cry-in-front-of-Chad!*

I could see what was happening. Though my head and body knew that Mark was no longer a part of me, my heart was not letting him off the hook so easily. For just a moment, I felt an ache so big I was afraid I might double over, and then Chad would think that either:

1.The butter I had been smearing on the breadsticks was rancid, or

2. I was engaging in some kind of weird prayer ritual.

No! No! No! I hid behind the menu and took a deep breath. "It's okay," I told myself. "You're okay." I had to realize that Mark would always be a part of me, but instead of feeling sadness, I could feel peace. I let the feeling wash over me and enjoyed it instead of trying to fight it off. In fact, lately, I had noticed that the feelings of pain and despair were being replaced with happy memories and an occasional laugh at a remembered private joke that would come to me at random times. I was okay. I lowered my menu to find Chad deeply engrossed in his.

Luckily, just then, the waitress appeared with another glass of chardonnay. Chad was still nursing his first beer. I ordered the blackened salmon with mashed potatoes, and Chad ordered grilled mahi with no butter and double vegetables. Uh oh. Could I learn to love a man who eats less than I do?

We made small talk during dinner about hobbies and work. I decided that since Chad had never been married—warning Will Robinson!— and had no children that he knew of, I would wait until our next date to fill him in on each of my adorable children, that I was sure, in time, he would come to love as his own.

The waitress reappeared and asked if we were interested in dessert.

"Oh, gosh no. I'm stuffed," I said, already thinking about the graham crackers and milk I would be enjoying later.

"Yeah," he said. "I have an early tennis match in the morning, so I probably need to call it a night."

That's okay, I thought. We have plenty of dates ahead of us, with so much more to discover. That freckle on my butt popped into my mind. Tingle. Tingle.

The waitress brought the check over and laid it on the table. Uh oh. What do I do? Do I offer to pay or just lay my card on the table? I bent down for my purse, but Chad reached for the bill and said, "Oh no, I've got it."

Once he signed the check and replaced his card in his wallet, he asked,

"Did you valet park?"

How sweet I thought, he probably wants to tip the valet guy for me.

"Yes, I did"

"Oh great, can you give me a ride to my car? I had to park like miles from here."

Of course, we all know what that means. He obviously can't wait to be alone with me.

"Sure, I'll take you."

The valet guy pulled up with my Toyota F-J and we both hopped in.

"Wow! This is a pretty big car. It's sort of more like a guy's car."

I didn't want to tell him it was either this or a mini-van. Anyway, we pulled up to his car and then it happened. He reached over and kissed me. Though this is what I had been wanting, I felt a little off guard. Where do I put my hands? Does my mouth smell like a wet salmon? Mmmmm, there was a little tongue action in there and though it felt weird at first, I liked it! I knew this could be the start of something special.

"Thanks!" he yelled and gave me a wave as he unlocked his car, a dark blue Jeep.

I drove home with a smile on my face, full of plans for Chad and me. Maybe I would invite him to the house for dinner one night when the kids were at Mark's. I could make that grilled swordfish with pineapple salsa that everyone used to love. Probably just fresh fruit for dessert, as I could see Chad liked to eat healthy. I think I still have that nice Morgan chardonnay in the fridge. Oh, and I can finally use my tie-dye napkins that I bought for a surprise birthday dinner for Stacy. Unfortunately, that never happened because her gynecologist invited her to her son's bar mitzvah on the same night, and I didn't have the heart to tell her that I had planned a special night for her that included colorful cloth napkins and a hunk of our favorite smoked gouda cheese. My mom said, "She's not giving up a night of dinner and dancing with the Schwartzes to sit on your patio eating chips and onion dip with a tie-dye napkin in her lap."

As soon as I closed the garage, I headed right for my computer. I logged onto my Match site and saw that Chad's light was on as well. He was probably waiting for me to log on, as well, so we could chat about our first date and make plans for our second.

I instantly typed, "Well, was I all that you thought I would be?"

Nothing. Nothing. Nothing.

I tried again. "I had fun. I think it was a success."

Finally, the little bleep went off that accompanied the iChat messages.

"Sorry. Just not feeling it."

And then his iChat light went from friendly green to *stop contacting me you stalker* red.

I gotta tell you, this one hurt.

Chapter 8: Hanging With the Girls

"Maybe our girlfriends are our soul mates and guys are just people to have fun with."—Candace Bushnell, Sex and the City

Soooooo? How was it? Did he love the peasant blouse?" I'd been dreading Stacy's call since I saw that little green light fade to blood red last night. First of all, to have the entire world know you'd been left by your husband for a gorgeous blonde was bad enough, but that at least made you, in a way, special. It causes a buzz in the neighborhood. People stop to look at you when you walk down the street thinking, "Gosh, she looks okay to me. I wonder why he did it." But *this*...this was going to leave people thinking, "Well there is obviously *something* about her that men find repulsive. Poor thing. Thank goodness she has pets."

I opened my mouth to tell Stacy my tale of woe, and I heard a big fat lie come out.

"Oh, um, he had a weird haircut and was kind of short. So, it's not gonna work for me."

"What? Well, what did you tell him when he asked for another date?"

"I just told him to call me, you know, then I just won't answer the phone and eventually he'll just have to get the hint."

"Wow!" There was real awe and admiration in her voice. I hated lying to my dearest friend, but I really saw no way around it.

The problem was, now that I'd had a little taste of it, meaning a man's tongue in my mouth, I wanted more. I was not ready to give up, but I was petrified of turning into that middle-aged woman who sits at the Bonefish bar, wearing a leopard print tank top on Bang-Bang Shrimp night, wobbling around on stilettos and over-laughing with the bartender.

However, lo and behold, a silver lining began to form. Even though I was having a rough go of it, two great things were happening. First, I gave up on the peasant blouse, and, second, something I had dreamed of my whole entire life was actually happening...I was becoming the *it* girl.

I began to notice it on a girls' night out. I think that I should explain what our girl's night out is. It's basically me, Stacy and three other neighborhood women drinking wine at our local sushi restaurant and talking about our husbands and kids. Let me further fill you in: If there's anything that can make a married woman, who starts her day by picking up her husband's dirty socks feel better about the chore, it's being around a newly divorced woman who has no one to pick her up if she has one too many cups of sake.

Sure, they had continued to include me in their little soirees, but that was mainly to make themselves feel better, and because Stacy insisted on it and she was the big ringleader. As soon as we'd get to Mr. Ikiro's, all the gals would flock around Stacy, telling her how awesome she looked and how they couldn't believe that fabulous lob she had in the tennis match, and then look over at me, sigh, drop their voice down an octave and say, "So, how are you doing? Any better?"

This time when Cathy asked me the question, Stacy piped up and said, "Amy's had two dates! Well, technically really one, I guess," and suddenly all eyes were upon me. This was it! This was the moment I had been dreaming of since junior high. No longer was I the nerd with the David Cassidy shag and uni-brow. Come on, I begged of myself, say something.

"I'll be right back, I have to pee."

Ugh, I couldn't blow it. I had to give them something I sat on the toilet, fully clothed, staring at a white plastic Buddha statue on the sink ledge and thinking of something to tell them that would give me an aura of mystery and sophistication, and not the aura of a woman who'd been dumped after just one dinner plate of salmon. I returned to the table, like Nora Desmond descending the stairs in *Sunset Boulevard* ready with my tale, but alas, it seemed my moment had passed. Everyone was talking about edamame and the Corona sushi roll, of which I told them to order three because it was my favorite. It has a wisp of lime on top—so freaking good.

I took my rightful seat on the corner where a chair had been wedged in for me and took a sip of my sake, which I have never liked and don't know why I drink it. Probably the same reason why I stole the *Monster Mash* forty-five from ABC Records in Tyrone Mall in 1973, because my friend Stacey told me to, and I have always, and probably will always, give in immediately to peer pressure. I realize it's a character flaw, but I can't help it. I think it's partly from an experience I had in seventh grade when Lee Gardner asked me if I smoke pot and I said no and he started pointing at me and yelling "Narc! Narc!" From then on I had to sit next to the kid who always wore a suit like the dad in *My Three Sons* and had a goatee like Charles Manson, even though he was only twelve, in the cafeteria, and, who, it turns out, was very nice. But still.

Conversation went from brown rice to inside-out rolls to extra wasabi to Cindy S. telling us about her son's little league game and then suddenly, Amy W. said, "I really love your son and I really love hearing about his games, but I would way rather hear about Amy's dates."

And just like that, I became the *It* girl of the moms in Eastlake Woodlands. I told them all about my first outing to the nasty Tiki bar and the now infamous red shawl. And then, maybe it was the sake or the mercury taking over my brain, I told them about Chad, and I mean the real story. Avery glanced at me from across the table but said nothing, and that's why I love her and pretend I don't care when her twins color with magic markers on my couch. Somehow, in the telling, I discovered that sharing the truth made the whole thing just an experience, not a tragedy that would define my life. Even more than that, I was laughing harder than I had ever since my divorce. In fact, I was having quite a bit of fun. It suddenly occurred to me, I like being around women. You know, they get me.

As I was beginning to emerge from the protective cocoon of husband and children, I realized there was much to be found in the company of women. When we began to dig a little deeper, when we started to pull from our depths, past the day-to-day trials and tribulations of husbands and kids, we found in each other warmth, empathy and ready listeners. Sure, there were a few bitches mixed in there as well, like Pam Atkinson who was naturally tan, weighed like ninety pounds, and was always talking about her au pair. But still, we could all relate. Most of us were in our mid- to late forties and knew a time was coming when there would be no more car pool lines, no more classroom holiday parties, no more checking homework, or packing back packs. We were all women preparing to face the next chapter of life. Many of us would be emerging as different people, when the daily duties of wife and mother began to fade away. Although some of us welcomed this new person, others were deathly afraid of who she might be. Still, we all knew there was no stopping her.

After coming clean with my pals, I began to feel a little more confident as I continued to navigate the online dating scene. One evening I logged onto my match account to see the new message light on. It turns out I had a "flirt" from—you're not going to believe this one—ERDoc4u. Here we go again folks.

I immediately checked his profile and liked what I saw. Greg had blonde hair and was wearing a polo shirt, the kind you would wear if you were a member of a ritzy golf club where men played billiards and women ate pimento cheese spread on tiny bread squares. In other words, not Jewish but a doc all the same.

Next to his profile it said "CURRENTLY ON LINE," so I instantly tuned in.

"Hi! Thanks for your flirt."

"My pleasure. Would you be interested in a phone call?"

"Wow, you don't waste any time."

"Well, I have very few nights away from the ER. Have to

make the most of them"

"Yes, I would be interested"

This one was the real deal. His name was Greg and he was an ER doctor at the local hospital having recently moved from Boston. He was divorced and had four children as well. Mentally I began trying to fit five more chairs around the dining room table.

We began to plan our first date.

"Do you like sushi?" he asked.

"Love it. I eat it like three times a week"

"You really shouldn't eat it that much, that is way too much mercury for you."

Tingle, tingle.

Due to his call schedule—did I mention he is an ER doctor—he had only one night available. Two days later, on a Friday evening, we made arrangements to meet at Vincenzo's, my favorite Italian place, where they put real anchovies into their Puttanesca sauce. I knew that Gabe was planning on spending the night out that Friday and Heather was going to her friend's beach house for the weekend. Turns out Heather had a friend whose parents were also divorced, only somehow this mom managed to wangle a Clearwater Beach condo out of the deal.

The first thing I had to do, of course, was call my mother.

"Mom, I don't want to get your hopes up, but I have a date with a doctor on Friday. A real one this time."

"Jewish?"

"Pretty sure, no,"

"No matter. Invite him for Thanksgiving. I'll make my chocolate chip pound."

Let's not forget that this conversation took place in September.

Speaking of mothers, let me interject a side note here about dating. As a mother, it sucks. Even if your date means you just sit at a Starbucks, watching the minutes pass, you wishing you had ordered the tall vanilla latte instead of the vente, because this ten minutes is lasting longer than the time you were on the exam table at your gynecologist's office and he said, "Can you wait here for a few minutes? I would like our intern to come in. He has got to see this!" Finally, you leave without saying more than hello and how nice it was to meet. Even so, when you walk into the house and see your kids, you feel like a dirty whore. At first. I don't know why this is, but it's something you have to work through.

Maybe it's because we want to shield our kids from seeing us as anything other than their mom. But in a divorce situation, there are other entities at play. In my case, their father was living with someone else on a daily basis. My kids never mentioned it, but I know at some level it has to eat at them. As mothers, we want our children to know that nothing will ever come before them. No other child, no man, no nothing—it has to be the one unwavering belief that carries them through life. I knew seeing their mother as a woman looking for love would be worse than the experience I had when I was five years old and ran into my kindergarten teacher, Mrs. Chef, in the grocery store. She was wearing pants. This scarred me for life.

Therefore, I never told my children when I was going on a date and tried to plan them for times when they were not at home. My friends said, "Why not? Be honest." I thought of giving it a try and even sat down and tried to put together the perfect thing to tell them, which went something like this: "Mommy is getting ready to go out on a date with a nice man who may be your next daddy. How do I look?"

See? Easier to just lie.

Anyway, that Friday, as I prepared for my date with Dr. Greg, I noticed myself feeling a little more self- assured and not quite as nervous as the first few times, probably due to the demise of the peasant blouse. I was not giving up on the jeans and espadrilles though.

I arrived at Vincenzo's a little bit early and immediately headed to the bar, like an old pro. I had eleven dollars all ready to go in my jeans pocket. I paid seven for my house chianti and left a four dollar tip, then sat at the bar pretending to be absorbed in my phone, even though the only text message I had was from Heather.

Just left for beach. Rudy pooped in office. Bye.

As I was sipping my chianti, an elderly gentleman approached me.

"Amy?" he asked, his eyes squinting from the light of the television.

Well, who could this be? Possibly friend of my father's who remembers me from a long time ago. He sort of looks like our neighbor, Mr. Mooney, who lived next door to us when I was eight. Could he possibly still be alive? He was like a gazillion years old back then.

"Yes?" I answered, already knowing in my churning gut who this is.

"I'm Greg!" he said.

"No," I wanted to say. "No, you're not. Greg has blond hair, not white. Greg does not wear high-waist jeans that have the crease ironed in. Greg does not wear dress shoes and socks with casual attire."

Guess what? He sure does.

I climbed off the bar stool, and Greg took my arm as the hostess brought us to a table. I'm not sure if it was to be gentlemanly or to steady himself as the restaurant was rather dark, and I'm sure he didn't want to stumble on our first date. In all seriousness, Greg was definitely closer to sixty than fifty.

We slid into opposite sides of the booth and just as he began to speak, his cellphone jangled. "Please excuse me for just one second, I really do have to talk to this patient. I'll keep it short. Promise."

What can I say? He has to talk to his patient. His patient. Because he's a doctor…

Suddenly, I began to warm up to him.

There is a lot an older man can bring to a relationship. Experience, wisdom, the ability to write prescriptions for anxiety meds. And anyway, what's so bad about a nice crisp crease in your jeans? God! Excuse the man for taking time for ironing after a busy day of saving lives.

After just a few minutes, he ended his conversation and directed all of his attention toward me, or should I say toward my boobs? Why of all times did I choose tonight to trade my beloved peasant blouse for a V-neck tee?

"Well, thank you for coming out with me on such short notice."

"Oh, well, I love this place."

A waitress appeared and laid down our menus.

"Would you like to order a cocktail?"

"Yes!" I barked. "I'll have a glass of your Chianti Classico."

"And I'll have a glass of your house chardonnay," said Greg.

What? Who drinks chardonnay with Italian food? Do men even drink chardonnay? Eww.

We began the usual chitchat—the weather, food likes and dislikes, his impression of Florida so far and, as I sipped on my chianti, I started to relax a little bit. *Don't be so judgmental!* I told myself.

Then we landed on the subject of kids, and I started to sort of like him. He seemed like a good father as he began to talk about his three sons and one daughter.

"So, where do they go to college?" I asked

"All four of them are in med school in Boston. Doing great. How about your kids? What are they into?"

Don't worry, I didn't tell him that they were running a drug cartel from our garage.

Anyway, by the time my Puttanesca and his lasagna arrived, he was half way through his second chardonnay. He looked at me and said, "So, have you been on a lot of these dates?"

"A few," I answered.

"Oh, how many have you had sex with?"

All right. Check please! I tried, I really tried, but this is not good.

"Oh, really nice," I said.

"Well, I've had sex with a few, and I have to tell you, just like I told them, should we get to that point, I have a very large penis."

I began slurping up my pasta so fast that I got hit in the eye with a piece of black olive. He, in the meantime, started in on his third chardonnay. He was still yammering on about his last girlfriend stalking him, and I wished she would show up right then and shoot him, not a mortal wound but maybe a flesh wound, which would give me time to get away.

"Can I interest you in dessert?" the waitress inquired.

Greg looked at me questioningly and I replied," No, I probably need to get going."

She then laid our check on the table and I waited for ERDoc to pick it up. Not happening. I grabbed my purse, pulled out my card and laid it on the little card tray and he did the same. "Shall we split it?" he asked.

"Sure," I replied. Just get me out of here.

With the bill paid, we made our way to the parking lot and panic began to bubble up in my chest along with a little Puttanesca. He was going to try to kiss me. I could just feel it. As I unlocked my car and climbed in, he stuck his head through my window, and I practically screamed,

"Don't put your head in here! My son spilled chocolate milk and it smells like throw up!" which, by the way, was not a lie.

I roared out of there as I heard him yell out, "We'll do this again soon. Right?"

Just for a moment, I tried to conjure up any latent lesbian tendencies. I once read an article that said seventy percent of women have lesbian desires, and I was really beginning to hope I was one of them. No woman I know would ever order chardonnay with Italian food. Plus, I would not have to be regaled with tales of their large penis. We could take turns cooking and share the laundry duties and just talk about stuff all the time. I would find a lovely woman like Ellen who would make me laugh, and we could live in her mansion in Hollywood where we would have Meryl Streep over for dinner, along with Brad Pitt, when Angelina was off on location. He would need to find a baby-sitter, though. I am not entertaining Viv, Shiloh and Pax the whole night.

At the thought of Brad Pitt, I felt that little tingle and realized the whole lesbian thing was not going to happen.

Ugh. It was already fall and the holidays were looming in front of me like one of our infamous Florida storm clouds, right before it lets loose with thunder and lightning that kills some old man walking around with a metal detector on the beach. As if facing my first officially divorced holiday season was not bad enough, I was sort of in a rut and knew I was going to have to make a change, career-wise. Not only was I not selling any homes, real estate was costing me a fortune between board fees, office fees, and replacing the lock box key that I left in a purse I had given to Goodwill. Let's not focus on the fact that some homeless woman is walking around carrying a fake Coach purse with a ripped lining and the ability to get into every home for sale in Florida.

One afternoon Stacy called me as I was putting together a dinner of chicken and broccoli cheese rice for the kids and she was preparing her infamous salmon bake. I could hear her opening her oven on the other end of the phone.

"I think we need a break. Let's go to a spa for a weekend," she suggested as I heard her oven door shut. You could barely hear it as she had the top of the line, Miele—a double with one convection.

"Right. I'll just tap into my vacation fund and take out a couple of thousand."

"Oh stop. Ken and I have a ton of miles. I'll cover the airfare. We'll split the hotel and you'll just have to ration your meals. Come on!"

I decided to go even though I hate spas. I hate walking around in a bathrobe. It reminds me of when my parents used to make us wear our pajamas to the drive-in movie and all the other kids were running to the snack bar dressed like normal people. I hate massages. That comes from the concrete knowledge that every masseuse man or woman, wants to have sex with me and will probably try without me even realizing it. I hate tiny plates of weird fruit and lemon water. Still, I felt a little break would be great for me. Plus Mark and OW were gearing up to decorate their home with a huge blow up Santa, eight reindeer and twinkly lights, and the kids were planning to help them over the weekend. They were so psyched, and, really, who could blame them?

I love being Jewish. It keeps me ever vigilant about any weird changes to my freckles and assures I will always lower my voice to a tiny whisper when I say the word *cancer*. No, seriously, it makes me feel part of something all protective and encompassing, and I feel peace in knowing my children are part of it as well.

It's just that during the holidays, being Jewish can kind of be a little bit of a downer. Just ride through the neighborhood and look at the lights, the Santas, the puffy Frosty the Snowmen. Then you pass a window with an electric menorah barely visible behind the drapes. Not quite the same effect.

As a Jewish woman who married a Catholic man, I thought I had the best of both worlds during holiday season. While the main floor of our home had a menorah and dreidels on the counter during the holidays, downstairs in the basement we had an entire winter wonderland. There was a tree, lights, music, and a dancing Santa. At sundown, we would run upstairs to recite our prayer and light a candle and then head back down for a joyful rendition of Rudolph. We were a family leading a double life. Now they could enjoy Christmas in the open.

Anyway, Stacy found a good deal at the Phoenician Spa in Arizona. This was ironic as Mark and I had had one of our best vacations there roughly fifteen years ago. I remember us lying in side-by-side chaises drinking Pina Coladas before my irritable bowel syndrome/lactose intolerance had kicked in. We hiked up Camel Back Mountain, and Mark made a cold compress for me with water and a handkerchief that he wrapped around my neck when I began to get overheated, about a quarter of the way up. He told me if you keep the back of your neck cool, your body would adjust, which was a little tip he learned in Ranger School. That night we had a fabulous dinner in our room where we drank a bottle of red wine and shared a piece of chocolate ganache cake. We promised each other we would try and do two alone trips a year. Would I still be avoiding OW and her stupid sundress in Publix if we had kept that promise?

I decided to give myself permission to spend the money needed to make this trip possible. In the scheme of things, it wouldn't keep me from feeding my children, and I felt it would be a great learning experience. I needed to know what it felt like to travel as a single independent woman, and, more importantly, I needed to know that I could do it. Now that I had mastered ordering a glass of wine in a bar all by myself, I felt up to the challenge.

We made plans to leave on a Thursday and return on Sunday. My first girls' trip. Since my marriage, other than an occasional visit to my sister in New York City, I had never traveled without Mark. Even those trips, which basically entailed a straight through flight and a cab ride, caused me great anxiety. Before getting on the plane, I would ask my sister exactly what to tell the cab driver to get me safely from La Guardia into her living room. I would then repeat it to myself over and over on the plane, leading my seatmates to believe I was either praying or a Rain Man. After I disembarked from the plane, I would make my way directly to the taxi line, Yellow cab only, muttering, "West 63rd between Columbus and Broadway." When the taxicab line guy finally directed me to my cab, I would walk up to the cabbie and scream, "West 63rd between Columbus and Broadway," into his face, much like a Tourette's patient.

I would let Mark know my whereabouts the entire time, "I'm on the plane," "I'm in the cab," "I'm eating pizza." This trip would be different. I had no one to report to.

The flight was great. Thanks to Stacy's sky miles, we sat right up in business class drinking Bloody Marys and discussing Stacy's spa treatments. Salt scrubs, seaweed wraps, and Swedish massages where a woman named Olga would beat the hell out of her. No thanks.

"Well what are you going to do while I'm out being loofahed?" Stacy asked.

"I don't know," I said pouring the last of my mini Stoli— how cute are those little things— into the Mr. and Mrs. T's mix. "Lay out at the pool," I guess.

"Oh, because you never get to do stuff like that at home,"

she replied.

"I may have a pool, but I don't lie around it."

In fact, I could not remember ever really being *in* it. I do remember sticking my foot into it after accidentally stepping on a lizard, but other than that...no. Mainly, I just liked staring into it when I was outside grilling flank steak.

After a nice, smooth landing, we took a cab to the resort and settled into our room. We immediately hit the pool and ordered some homemade potato chips and bleu cheese dip. Heaven. After that, we made a reservation for dinner in the organic farm restaurant. It turns out when you go out to dinner with a woman, it's perfectly fine to order two salads instead of an entree. I couldn't decide between the arugula salad with the artichoke vinaigrette and the Caprese with home grown tomatoes. I had both. For dessert, what else? We shared the cheese plate and a piece of fresh peach cake. What man would do that?

In the morning, Stacy headed down for her first treatment of the day, and I ordered coffee and oatmeal in the room. As I was licking off the last of the brown sugar from the rim of my bowl, Stacy returned virtually gleaming from her salt scrub.

"I just made a reservation for an astrology reading. You have to come with me! If you send him your birth date and time, he can do yours today, too."

"Why? That stuff freaks me out. I don't want to know when I'm going to die or what type of cancer I'm going to get."

"No, he's not a fortune teller. He reads your astrological chart. And I don't remember anything from my childhood and you remember everything, so I need you to be there.

"Fine, but I'm not wearing a bathrobe."

At four-thirty that afternoon, we were sitting in the little waiting area where everyone else but me had on a terry cloth robe. It reminded me of the waiting room at the mammogram facility that causes me night terrors.

Suddenly, a man appeared from a side door.

"Mrs. M?"

"Yes," we both answered.

"Actually, she's Mrs. M, but she wants me to come in with

her because she doesn't remember anything," I explained.

"Well, it's a very small room, but I suppose we can find a space for you."

Once again, I was the belle of the ball.

Astrologer Tim led us past rooms with massage tables reeking of eucalyptus to a tiny room with a small table and two chairs and directed Stacy to sit in one of them. He pointed to a little stool in the corner where I planted myself. He began looking at Stacy's chart and making comments.

"You have many amazing opportunities opening up to you very soon."

"Good for you, Stacy."

"Shhh," Tim instructed me.

"I can see here that both of your parents are deceased and I can see that you had a very close bond with your mother. How was the relationship between you and your father?"

"Great!" Stacy answered.

"What? He always called us idiots."

In fact, Stacy's dad was hilarious and I have very fond memories of him, but he did call us idiots sometimes.

Another glare from Tim shut me up and I checked out for a while.

I came back when I felt the reading was ending and Tim was wrapping it up.

"You are very smart, your mind is amazing and you are capable of great things. I feel like perhaps you should try writing a novel. If you decide to go back into law, you will most likely make be a powerful force and cause great change within society. Also, you should know your children will follow in your footsteps. They will make you very proud."

With that he gave Stacy a hug and we switched places.

My turn. I was actually looking forward to my reading now. I could see that Stacy felt energized and optimistic from hers. Here was a professional, um, astrologer telling her that there was a whole life waiting for her when she was done with the daily duties of motherhood. Not only that, but she could rest assured that her children were on the right path and were going to be hugely successful. I couldn't wait for him to tell me about the fabulous career awaiting me and the amazing things *my* children were going to accomplish.

He began, "Unfortunately, I didn't have enough time to do a complete chart for you, so I'm not going to charge you but will give you a few highlights from what I do see."

He looked down at my chart and said, "Now, you are very smart too, but in a *special* way. I see you as more of a creative person. Have you ever tried sewing? Maybe you should take up quilting or something."

"Oh, well, I hadn't really thought about that," I said.

"Well you definitely should," Tim instructed.

"What about my children?" I asked.

He looked down at the chart again and said, "They'll probably be fine." With that we said our good-byes and headed for the pool.

The remainder of the trip was filled with sunbathing, shopping, eating, drinking and laughing. I found it wonderful just being. There was no agenda, no time we had to be anywhere, no need to jam every moment with some type of activity. Silences did not need to be filled. We went into a cool kitchen store and bought funky porcelain chopsticks and funny refrigerator magnets and quirky salad tongs shaped like hands. If we got hungry, we ate. If we wanted a nap, we slept. We were on our own, but together. It was not only fabulous, it was eye-opening.

On the flight home, we were less jubilant knowing we were returning to our day-to-day existence. Still we laughed about Tim and our readings and sighed deeply when we thought about those damn homemade potato chips.

For me, the trip was more than just a weekend away. It was a life-changing experience. I began to see that the relationships I had with the women in my life—Stacy, my sisters, even the Sushi restaurant moms—were more than just a way to fill time until I found a man to share my life with. They were more than a reason to have a glass of wine and split a decadent dessert on a Tuesday night. These were the people who would sustain me as I embraced my future, which would apparently be filled buying discount fabric at Allen's Craft Store and watching my children be fine.

Chapter 9: A Divorcee Impresses Her Friends

"Bah! Humbug!"—Scrooge

It was now late November and, just as I had predicted, my official holiday/unemployed/really bad haircut slump was in full swing. I was job hunting—again—and not really having a whole lot of luck. I told myself it was because it was holiday time and not because I was old, had no college degree and no real job experience. To add to this dilemma, Tim, my hair stylist, had talked me into a new asymmetrical haircut. Basically, on the left side of my face, my hair was chin length and, on the other side, it was cut over my ear. I felt sort of lop-sided and was starting to walk with my naked ear pressed to my shoulder, kind of like Marty Feldman in *Young Frankenstein*. I knew it was a mistake when I was getting up from his chair and Tim said, "The great thing about hair is it always grows back."

I had also been on another date. This time with a real jokester. We met at Cheesecake Factory at International Mall, which was dangerous territory for me because I knew that Mark and OW liked to dine at the Capitol Grill over there, and it was just a matter of time before I ran into them. With my luck, it would be on my first date with a man who claimed to be five-foot ten, but was, in fact, four-foot ten. I could just see Mark in all of his six foot two glory saying, "Well now, who is this little fella," with OW standing there in one of her sundresses, her blonde hair whipping in the wind while she stared at the shaved side of my head.

Anyway, I am going to spare you the details of this debacle

other than to say this guy had such a great sense of humor and thought it was really funny to change tables every time I went to the bathroom. I would come out of the bathroom and not see him and think, *Thank you Jesus for making him disappear.* Then, out of the corner of my eye, I would see him at another table laughing at me. He was a hoot, aka, a fucking idiot.

On this particular Wednesday afternoon, I was just about to engage in the highlight of my day, which coincidentally was also my exercise: getting the mail from my mailbox. This involved me walking to the end of the driveway with my head down so as to avoid conversation with neighbors who were also walking with their heads down to avoid conversation with me. I reached in and pulled out the usual assortment of bills and coupons and then, lo and behold, I saw something unique. A party invitation! Cathy was throwing a holiday party at her home the second week in December and Amy Koko plus guest was invited.

Now here's the thing about me and holiday parties. I love them. I love getting invited to them and I love the days leading up to them when I run around looking for that perfect necklace or new lipstick to complement my outfit, which, don't worry, will not be including a peasant blouse. I love imagining myself surrounded by party guests, all eyes glued to me, listening to my latest anecdote with bated breath. "And so I told Simon and Schuster as well as Penguin and Harcourt, look, I really think I will be way better off self-publishing, but thank you so much for your interest and your out-of-this-world advance offers. And then of course, Julia Louis Dreyfuss was quite disappointed when I told her I had no intention of turning my self-published e-book into a movie but thanked her profusely for her interest..."

The day of the party I will spend primping, bathing in scented oils, which will invariably lead to some type of itchy infection in my lady parts but is well worth it, shaving, plucking and bleaching. I will leave it to your imagination to figure out what happens where. I oil up my arms and legs. My body refers to this as its annual moisturizing, and dress with care. One final look and I am off for a night of fun, excitement and even possible romance.

Finally, the moment arrives. I enter the party, greet the host and hostess—kiss, kiss—and make my way to the bar. The bartender hands me a glass of chardonnay, which I take, and make a beeline for a quiet corner by the heavy drapes. I then turn and face the wall. It's always this moment when I remember my self-diagnosed social anxiety disorder and my dislike of large groups of people all wearing sweaters with embroidered Christmas trees on them, some with real ornaments. Seriously, this happens every time.

P.S. I love my Christian friends, but you guys, the sweaters...WHY?

The other problem facing me was the "Plus Guest" part of the invite. The only thing worse than not having a guest to bring to a party is your host supplying one for you. This might result in you sitting next to the hostess' husband's cousin Leo, who owns a lighting store in the gross part of Tampa and tells you he, too, is divorced and that his ex-wife is a bitch, "A real *See You Next Tuesday*, if you know what I mean," and then starts to cry while shoveling stuffed mushrooms into his mouth.

As I was contemplating the situation, Stacy called. "Did you get the invite?" she asked eagerly.

"Yeah, I got it, but I don't think I'm gonna go."

"What? Why? You'll come with me and Ken. We'll pick you up and take you. It's gonna be so fun. Come on."

Now, I had been on a lot of "dates" with Stacy and Ken in the last year. This involves me sitting in the back seat of their car while they make quiet married talk in the front. Every once in a while I stretch my head into the front seat and say, "What?" and they say, "We were saying how much fun tonight is going to be," and I feel like I did when I was six years old in the back of my parents car, only this time I'm wearing a seat belt.

"I'll think about it," I said.

And I did think about it. I had an idea. I would bring a guest, and I had the perfect guest in mind—Dr. Greg. Now, hold on. You're asking the same question my editor did when she sent this part back all lined out and wrote, "No one will believe you. And if it is true, what's wrong with you?"

Let me explain. Yes, he had white hair. Yes, he wore ironed jeans. And, yes, he talked about his penis. But he was a doctor, and I wanted to impress my friends. Imagine me entering the party not standing between Stacy and Ken like one of their twins, but with a real date, and a doctor no less. Not only would I not be a third wheel again, but I would be perceived as a confident divorcee with an interesting man on my arm. I could envision my friends asking him about bio-identical hormones and their husbands' cholesterol levels. He would be holding court, regaling the crowd with tales of the ER and his life saving heroics. How bad could he be? Perhaps I had judged too harshly. I told myself that he was nervous the night we went out, thus the three chardonnays and penis talk. Another bonus—the party was a dressy occasion, so it would be okay that he wore his black shiny dress shoes. Yes, it was all falling into place.

I logged onto my Game Set Match.com account and, of course, he was online. It appeared that when he wasn't saving lives he was looking for a date. I wrote:

Remember me?
Of course. How are you? Get that car cleaned?
Yes. Question for you
Yes??????
Would you like to come to a neighborhood holiday party with me?
When is it?
Saturday December 16
Love to
You can pick me up and we will go together
I am honored
I will text you more details later

There was a little rumble in my stomach after that exchange, the kind that means I had one too many cheese enchiladas or I had a bad feeling about something I was about to do. Unfortunately, both led to the same results, and I had plenty of private time in the bathroom to mull it over.

I replied back to Cathy.'s invitation and said I would be attending with a guest. Instantly the entire community—okay my three friends and Stacy—were abuzz with who this guest would be. I simply told them a doctor I met on Game Set Match.com and left it at that. This would add an air of mystery to my already growing *It* girl persona.

I then began to think about my holiday party outfit and also about the holiday gift list I had received from my children. My children are kind, sweet, and sensitive, but, starting December 1st, they turn into spoiled Christmas brats. Mackenzie goes from telling me, "Don't tell me to always carry cab money. I am an adult you know?" to sending me the following list:

Hi Mommy!! Here is my holiday gift list!

New patent Steve Madden boots, and get them from his website, not Shoe Carnival. Let's not have a repeat of the Doc Martens episode from seventh grade please.

Lots of MAC make up - No-Wait! Just a gift card, I better pick out my own stuff

A NutriBullet - you wouldn't believe how much money I am spending at the juice bar Any clothes from the website I directed you to for my birthday except-oh never mind, just do a gift card here too

Now, that's one out of four, and the other lists were just as long. Basically, this meant I would be shopping for my holiday party outfit in my own closet. Shopping in my closet is sort of like shopping at TJ Maxx seconds after they receive a shipment of last year's Donna Karan at 75% off —a freaking free for all. I'm a closet slob, and I admit it. I start out every new closet really good, with my shoes all paired up and the heels pointing outwards. One year later, the only shoes I really wear, my Reef flip-flops, are kept next to my bed, and none of the shoes in the closet have mates anywhere near each other. My disorganization led to a horrible accident when I accidentally washed an UGG boot with my towels when I scooped them all up off the closet floor and threw them in the machine. It came out looking like a wet cat. Also, my T-shirts, which started out folded and color coordinated, are rolled up into little balls and stuffed anywhere there is an opening. There is a variety of wrapping paper left over from eight Hanukahs ago and a plethora of purses including an army green Nine West messenger bag from 1996 that I never did have the balls to wear, but know will come in handy one day.

This particular morning, one week before the big event, I entered the hellish scene with a big mug of coffee and began to peruse the merchandise. I decided to shop in the cocktail dress section, which basically included four black dresses in various lengths, including one that was long and tight around my ankles making me look like a chubby Morticia Addams who walks like a geisha. Then I saw the dress I had worn to Mackenzie's Bat Mitzvah about nine years ago. It was black with spaghetti straps made of gold chain and pearls. I tried it on with a full body Spanx and not only was it passable, it looked pretty good. Oh my God, I would be positively stunning in my first social outing as an accompanied divorcee. Now this is going to really up my status!

The morning of the party I texted Dr. Greg my address, once again noticing that foreboding rumble in the gut. For this special evening, I decided to disobey the first rule of online dating and let Dr. Greg pick me up at my home. I wanted to be driven like a lady, not make a rendezvous spot where we would meet up and then have him follow me to the party like some creepy stalker.

Later in the morning, Deb called to check in and tell me she was having a pre-party gathering at her house and wanted us to be there.

"Who else is coming?" I asked.

'Just you guys and the Rosenbaums, which will be great because Michael is a doctor, too."

Well,this really was shaping up into the perfect night. *My* doctor would sit and converse with another doctor while wife Phyllis and I talked about horrendous call schedules and the bitchy nurses who were always after our men. I felt bad for Stacy, knowing she would probably feel a little left out. I mean,

Phyllis and I were with doctors. Stacy's husband only owned his own finance company and had been written up in the Tampa Times as the official whiz kid of our generation, but I would try to make a point of keeping her engaged. She's been such a good friend, after all.

That evening, after my day of the earlier described prep work, I stood by the front door in my black cocktail dress, wearing my old Jimmy Choo's, a gift from Mark given to me somewhere between the announcement of OW and his intent to never see her again and the decision that they should live together on the same street as me, and carrying a little black evening bag from Target, which, by the way, is my new go-to for purses.

Eventually, I saw headlights creeping up my street as though the car was using a walker. He even drove old. With his dome light on, Dr. Greg squinted through his reading glasses, trying to make out house numbers just like my grandfather did when my parents were on vacation and he had to drop me off at a birthday party in sixth grade. Gross. The instant he pulled into my driveway, I was there to meet him, to prevent his car from driving even an inch closer to my house. I pulled at the door handle several times while he fumbled to unlock it.

"Wow, you look great," he said, squinting at me under the car dome light.

Although Dr. Greg was dressed appropriately in khakis with no crease that I could see and a light blue dress shirt, I knew I had made a fatal mistake. He was old. I could never kiss him. His hands looked veiny. I told myself, "Those hands may have saved lives today," and that made me feel a little better, but I knew he had to have old man toenails and that this was going no further.

"Thanks. Thanks for picking me up."

"No problem. I know where you live now."

Eww! Oh no. I have put my entire family in grave danger in order to impress my friends at a party. I wonder how impressed they will be when they find my head floating around in Lake Tarpon. I can hear it now, with my friends all gathered around, "He seemed so nice and so intelligent. He probably just snapped, I mean let's face it, she can get on anyone's nerves after a while..."

I told him, "My friend is having a little get together before the party, so we will go to her house first. It's just around the corner here."

"Okay, that sounds great. Just tell me where to go..."

How about away...just...away.

We began the slow crawl to Stacy's making small talk about the neighborhood, and, I have to say, I perked up quite a bit when I noticed a prescription pad in the center console of his jeep. Therein lay the end to my anxiety, irritable bowel syndrome, occasional eczema and weight gain. Yes, there's a pill for that now. So what if they cause heart failure? We arrived at Stacy's and he came around and opened the door for me. Nice touch. We rang the bell and Stacy greeted us with open arms.

"Hi Stacy, this is Greg.

"Hi Greg, it's so great to meet you. Come in. This is my husband Ken"

Ken introduced himself to Greg and they headed off to the kitchen. Stacy pulled me aside, "How old did you say he was?" she demanded.

"Late fifties. Shut up. He's a doctor."

We joined the men in the brightly lit gourmet kitchen, where Ken was mixing up a big batch of Cosmopolitans. The Rosenbaums were already seated in the living room where the four of us joined them, all of us carrying our sexy martini glasses—the ones with the faces on them that Stacy had picked up at Z Gallery. Once again introductions were made as we settled ourselves around on the chocolate brown leather couch. The two doctors were making conversation; everything was going smoothly. I sipped my Cosmo, just starting to feel that warm inner glow when all of a sudden, Dr. Greg slurped up the rest of his Cosmo, placed his empty glass on the coffee table and picked up the small plate of nuts that had been put there for us all to enjoy. He placed it in his lap and began to eat them as though it was his last meal. Conversation continued around him while he threw one nut after another into his mouth chewing like a camel.

"Would you like another drink?" Ken, ever the quintessential host, asked him.

"Sure." replied Dr. Greg.

Stacy and I exchanged looks. Hers said, "You are a fucking idiot. What were you thinking," and mine said, "I saw his prescription pad!"

Ken returned with Dr. Greg's second drink. It was hard to continue casual conversation as we listened to Dr. Greg inhale an entire plate of peanuts and then gulp down his Cosmo in three swallows. With each obscenely loud crunch, I knew not only were my friends not impressed with my date, but that they were probably very grossed out. He held his glass up, "Can you top me off?" he asked Ken.

Okay, I deserved this. This is what you get for trying to be the cheerleader/homecoming queen when deep down you know you belong on the debate team. I gave Ken an evil glare as he stood up to retrieve the good doctor's glass.

Finally, Dr. Greg finished the peanuts *and* his third Cosmo and it was time to leave for the real party.

"We'll just follow you guys," I yelled as we all loaded up into our cars.

"That was great! Really great," Dr. Greg said as we started the caravan.

"You better watch it with your drinking," I said. "You still have to drive yourself home tonight. And slow down. We have deer in here you know."

He was no longer driving like my grandfather. He was driving like someone trying to evade the police.

"Well that's okay. If I get too drunk I can just stay at your house."

"Uh, no you can't. I have kids. That will never happen. Just watch yourself."

"I think I know why you're divorced," he answered.

Oh my God, I hate him. Not only that, I began to get a little scared. How in the world was I going to get rid of him now? He had to drive me home. What if he wouldn't leave? What if he made a scene out in my driveway? What if he held me hostage in my own home? I began to think of ways to signal to my neighbors through the windows that I needed help. Fuck, they all hated me because of the time our illegal generator kicked on during a storm and blew out all the electricity in the neighborhood. They were without power for three days while our generator kept on running to the sound of about a hundred Harleys, our house lit up like a swimwear dressing room at Macy's. No, they wouldn't help me. I also realized I did not have a will and I had left no instructions for my children should I be on a ventilator, like if he doesn't kill me all the way, just tortures me for days and shoots me up with all kinds of weird drugs. I want them to know to not pull the plug on me.

Yeah, that's right. I do not want my plug pulled. Who knows, I still may snap out of it. I do not carry a DNR card; I carry a card that says, "Resuscitate, bitches!" I want my kids to come see me every day, make sure I am still hooked up to Netflix and HBO to GO, and check that my DVR is recording Real Housewives and Project Runway. Is it asking so much? That after all I have done for them, they continue to see to my television needs? They say you can still hear when you're in a coma, you just can't speak. Great! No interruptions.

If I group texted the kids right now and just said if anything ever happens to me don't pull the plug, would that alarm them? My kids? Probably not. I would be more likely to get a text back saying, "But did you leave dinner?"

We pulled up to the party and parked behind a row of cars lining the street. I could see through the light- filled windows that the party was in full swing, the giant puffy Santa welcoming us in, Jingle Bell Rock wafting through the night air. I opened my own car door and went to step out of the car. That is when I felt it —the strap on my dress broke, sending little pieces of gold chain and pearls skittering onto the sidewalk, and almost leaving my whole right boob exposed. Stacy came up to me and I looked at her panic-stricken,

"Oh God. The strap on my dress just broke."

By this time Dr. Greg had stumbled his way over to my side of the car. "What happened?" he slurred.

"The strap on my dress just broke."

He looked leeringly at my chest, weaving from foot to foot and said, "Well if ya didn't...if ya didn't...if ya didn't have such big gazongas!"

Oh Jesus, Mary and Joseph, Moses, Abraham and Anne Frank, did a medical professional just call my breasts gazongas? Does he tell his female patients to make sure and have their yearly gazongagram? Does he call vaginas, vajongas? This is a doctor? Is this my payback for making fun of that girl with kinky red curly hair and hammer thumbs in junior high school? Karma is a bitch and all of that?

"Well, just hold onto it. We'll go into the bathroom and fix it," Stacy assured me. " I'm sure Cathy will have a safety pin or tape or something."

We made our way up to the door with Dr. Greg weaving closely behind. Cathy, the hostess greeted us. Beyond her I could see people milling about, talking, laughing, everyone carrying tiny plates piled high with mini quiches and brie puffs. A huge Christmas tree twinkled in the corner with presents already piled high underneath it. A fake fire roared in the Florida fireplace. The air smelled of pine, clove and mini hotdogs in barbeque sauce, all smells I loved. My favorite holiday song, *Baby It's Cold Outside*, began pouring through the speakers. Sweaters aside, this was a great party. I would have really enjoyed being there alone with my friends, I thought. I promised God if he just got me through this night alive and not too embarrassed, I would never try and impress people again. I would just be myself, a single woman who dates a married couple.

"Hi Cathy, this is Greg. My dress strap just broke. Do you have a little pin?"

"Sure," she said pulling one from a very organized kitchen drawer. "Here you go. Make yourself at home, Greg," she said. "The bar is over there and dinner is in the kitchen, dessert is laid out in the dining room."

"Okay," he said and headed for the bar. Surprise, surprise.

Stacy and I made our way to the bathroom. "Oh my God. What am I going to do?"

"It's fine. We'll just pin it."

"No, idiot, I mean about my date, this night. This hell I am in."

"Oh, that. Yeah, that part does really suck. Just get through it, I guess. Now we know not to invite your dates to parties where there may be people who are not alcoholics."

"Shut up. And check on me tomorrow. If you don't reach me by noon, send the forensics unit over."

She left the bathroom to join the party and have some fun with her husband and less pathetic friends. I decided to face-time my sister who was in California shooting an opening segment for Monday Night Football with the Rolling Stones.

She answered after a few rings, "What's wrong?" she demanded when she came into focus. I could see wires, cameras and lots of people in black T-shirts and jeans running around in the background.

"Nothing, I'm at a party and my date is drunk and old."

"Ick. That sucks."

"Yeah."

"How's the food?"

"Looked pretty good. They have those mini barbeque hot dogs."

"Any Rumaki? I love Rumaki."

"What? No one makes Rumaki anymore. That went out with Swedish meatballs."

"Oh. Too bad. Let me see what you're wearing." I heard a male voice from somewhere off camera calling her name. "Hold on! I'll be right there! You'd think he was Mick Jagger or something. Oh wait, it *is* Mick."

I panned down so she could see my ensemble.

"Wow, you can still fit in the dress from Mackenzie's Bat Mitzvah?"

"I think so. Does my ass look huge?" I aimed the camera at my butt.

"No, it looks okay. But look, I need to get back before Keith Richards passes out, so just enjoy the hot dogs wherever it is you are and I will call you in a few days when I get back."

With that the screen went black. It was time to face the music.

I regretfully emerged from the bathroom and out of etiquette and decorum decided to join my date. I looked around and saw nothing but happy people in ugly sweaters, one even had working jingle bells on it, laughing and enjoying themselves. *Merry Little Christmas* was now wafting through the air and I started to feel a bit melancholy. That changed to a mix of sheer embarrassment and disgust when I saw Dr. Greg walking around sloshing a drink onto the floor with one hand and carrying an entire plate of mini brownies in the other. He had apparently taken the entire top plate of a three tiered dessert tray for himself. This humiliation was worse than what I had endured the time five-year-old James was taking swimming lessons and came up from the water yelling to his teacher who was like sixty years old, "Hey, you farted!"

It became clear to me that this was not going to end well. I began to contemplate my fate as I made my way over to the mini hot dogs, the one highlight of my evening. As I was chewing my first one and getting ready to shove in the next one, my friend Kate came up to me. I like Kate a lot. She's smart, doesn't judge me, and has very nice hair.

"Hi Amy, how's it going?" she asked.

"Have you seen my date? And if so, do you really need to ask?"

"Yes, I saw him. Um, what's that about?

"He's a doctor."

"Oh, okay. That explains it. I will never get what it is with you Jewish girls and doctors. Especially drunk ones."

"Yeah, I think I learned my lesson this time."

We were in the midst of a conversation about Cathy.'s living room walls, which for some reason were painted a dark pink, when a strange man came up to me and tapped me on the shoulder.

"Huh?" I turned around to face him.

"Um, I think your date is asleep."

"What?" I turn to see Dr. Greg passed out on the couch, chin lying on his chest. A Santa hat was perched atop his head and people were heaving grapes from the fruit bowl at him. It really felt like it was time for me to go home.

"Oh my God!" I said to Kate, near tears by now. "I can't deal with this. I have to get out of here."

"And I am ready to take you," she answered.

I quickly said my good-byes to Cathy and apologized profusely to her. Ken kindly volunteered to put my snoring date in a cab.

As Kate and I made our way to the front door, out of the corner of my eye I saw the couch with Dr. Greg asleep on it being lifted up and carried onto the golf course, which was right behind Cathy's house.

We made the short drive to my house, and on the way we both began to laugh hysterically. This is one that will go on record and be told over and over for many girls' nights to come. Plus, I learned it is better to be alone than to be with a raging asshole, even if he does have a prescription pad.

I got out of the car and thanked Kate profusely.

"It's nothing, but please...no more doctors. They are obviously not all they are cracked up to be."

Safely inside, I took off my makeup and decided there was only one way to deal with the broken dress. I threw it in the outside trash; I did not want that karma following me around. I cleaned my face, brushed my teeth, poured myself a big bowl of cereal, and got into bed with my recordings of Project Runway.

Within minutes my phone began to buzz incessantly, and I saw that it was Dr. Greg. I turned it off and gave Tim Gunn and Heidi my full attention.

The next morning I awoke early and turned my phone on to find a text message from the good doctor:

Where is my car?

I texted him Cathy's address and put him out of my mind forever.

P.S. Two weeks later I received the following text:

Amy I'm really sorry about the other night. I can usually handle my liquor, don't' know what happened. Anyway, just wondering...what are you doing for New Years?

Chapter 10: Period. End of Story.

"Estrogen deficient women are the walking dead."—Maria Hoag, MBA

Mid-February finds me making my yearly trek to Dr. Annabelle Weiss's office, my beloved gynecologist, and I dread it. Being the huge cancer-phobe that I am, I approach any type of medical check-up with the same level of fear most people reserve for, say, waking in the middle of the night to find a strange man standing over their bed with an axe, or the oxygen masks dropping down midflight. I know it's weird, but as much as I love doctors as possible husband material, I hate seeing them in a professional capacity. They scare the shit out of me.

I pull up to the office with a list of questions for Dr. A.W., all memorized in my head:

1. Is there still, in fact, a vagina even down there?
2. In the last few months, I have noticed I cannot pee without farting — what's that about?
3. Why is my hair thinning and my mustache coming in better than ever?
4. Where are my eyebrows?
5. Really, how much alcohol is too much alcohol and so what, I can stop any time I want.

I also wanted to ask her for birth control pills to regulate my period, which had been showing up either every week or not at all. Weird.

I tug open the door to the office and am greeted by a myriad of shining happy faces and big bellies. The preggos are all talking amongst themselves:

"We're having a boy and are thinking either Luke, Josiah or Declan," said obvious homeschooler.

"Yes, the midwife will come to the house and we will have the birth in the living room because my grandmother can't climb the stairs."

"We're due on the 28th. We planned it to coincide with our dog Bentley's birthday!"

I make my way to the back of the waiting room where the middle-aged women are silently sitting with their purses in their laps reading Fosamax brochures. I sit and try to act normal as if this is no big deal, as if I am not about to have someone reach their hand up into my bodily orifices and feel around for cancerous masses. I don't remember exactly when I became afflicted with this phobia, but I do know that it has made me do some very inappropriate things, like calling Dr. A W. in the middle of the night to tell her I just found a lump in my neck. It turned out to be an ingrown hair, and frankly, I'm not sure which is scarier, possible cancer or hair growing on my neck. Then there was the time I spent two days tracking down my dermatologist's home phone number on her day off for the results of my skin biopsy. Final diagnosis: Weird rash.

Unfortunately, this obsession bled over into my mothering skills as well, and I tended to take every little symptom, be it sore throat or stomachache, to the unthinkable extreme. I had a terrible scare one afternoon, when Gabe was two, over a swollen lymph node sticking out under his ear. With my heart pounding out of my chest, I threw him in the car and made the usual 20 minute trip to the pediatrician in ten-minutes. What I thought was a deadly case of childhood leukemia turned out to be a raging case of impetigo, apparently contracted when he was playing in our koi pond and then ate his lunch without washing his hands. "Impetigo," Doctor John explained, "is an infection from dirt." I stared at him lovingly as relief began to flow through my body. "What?" I asked.

"Yes, you know," he continued, "from being dirty. From not washing."

I felt like the mother in *Coal Miner's Daughter*.

"But gosh dang it, Doc," I wanted to say. "I do the best I can with these four young'uns. Washin', ironin', schoolin' 'em all by my darned self." Forget about their father and the private school. That was beside the point.

Now, sitting here in the doctor's office, waiting to be called in to the inner sanctum, I thought back to all the stuff I had read lately regarding women's health issues. Indigestion is a sign of ovarian cancer? Oh God! I have indigestion sometimes. Bloated stomach means ovarian cancer? No! I was bloated three nights ago. True, I had finished off a liter of diet soda, but still, this warrants investigation. My heart was beating out of my chest and sweat had gathered along my hairline and butt crack.

The side door opened, "Ms. Koko?"

"Right here."

"Come on back."

I was weighed, had my blood pressure taken, and asked to leave a urine specimen. I was then hustled into a room with the dreaded stirrup table and a paper towel with a glob of jelly plopped on it, sitting on the counter. This was really bad. Next year I was going to have to take a Xanax, drink a glass of wine and come by cab. Have to.

Once I had my paper gown on I climbed onto the table and began to position myself. It was always so awkward when Dr. A.W. would say from down at the end of the table, "Come down a little more, a little more...more..." with the paper loudly scrunching up into my butt as I wriggled my way down towards her. This year I wanted to be ready.

Finally, there was that little knock on the door that doctors always gave. What are they afraid they're going to walk in on? What could be going on? We have been sitting there for at least fifteen minutes, trying to hear what is going on in the other rooms, haven't we? Haven't we? Come in and let's get this damn thing over with, already.

"How are you?" Dr. A.W. says as she breezes in and washes her hands.

"Pretty good," I say, trying to keep a normal voice.

Dr. A.W. keeps up a string of conversation as she runs her fingers along my neck and checks my breasts for lumps. She then takes a seat at the end of the table, turns on a light strong enough to illuminate the entire stage at an Aerosmith concert, and begins to insert what feels like a military vehicle into my vagina.

Suddenly, I see a frown form between her eyes, which is all I can see of her from my angle.

Oh God...tumor!

She lets out a sigh. "Next year would you please remind me to use the extra-long speculum?"

Mental note to Google "extra-long speculum."

Finally, Dr. A.W. rolled her chair back, snapped off her rubber gloves and said, "So, do you have any questions or concerns for me?"

"Yeah, I was thinking I might need to go on birth control pills because my periods have been so weird, you know, like they come every week or then they might wait two months before showing their face again."

"How old are you now?" Dr. A.W. said, as she glanced at my chart.

"Forty-seven," I answered, and suddenly I knew what was coming.

"Birth control pills?" she snorted. "You don't need birth control pills, but you might need hormones. You're in menopause."

"What? No way. Already?"

"Well, fifty-two is the average age, but these symptoms can appear both prior and after that age, including irregular periods, and the weight gain."

"Weight gain?"

"Yes, it looks like you've gained about six pounds since last year. You should really think about beginning to watch your diet and starting an exercise program. Do you exercise at all now?" she asked, daring me to say yes.

"I take my dog for a very long walk every day, so, yeah, I exercise."

"Well, let me put it to you like this. At this stage, you have to do at least one hour of cardio exercise every day just to maintain where you are. One Hour. To Maintain."

Is there no end to this hell? Here's basically what I see happening. My husband is leaving me for a young blonde pastry chef. I'm not getting my outdoor kitchen, and now generic Pop Tarts are a special occasion dessert. Deal with it. I'll be seeking some type of work that will probably require coffee preparation and learning to use the copy machine. It's probably just a matter of time before I move to one of those divorcee condos where everyone lies around the pool in bathing suit cover-ups drinking vodka and orange juice from a thermos. Now on top of that, I'm expected to exercise one hour a day, actively, in order to hold on to the body that's basically already totally disgusting. I mean, really, who is in charge around here? I would like to file a complaint.

Dr. A.W. said her goodbyes as she left me with one more happy thought regarding menopause.

"Diet and exercise are the only way through it. Otherwise things can get bad, real bad. See you in a year," she chirped, and was gone.

Menopause. Or as I thought of it: THE END. Who would ever want me now? I'm done. Finished. How would I ever entice a man to be with me intimately again? I could see us kissing passionately, and then he takes my hand and leads me into the bedroom. "Hold on one minute, I just have to squirt a gallon of lube into my vagina, then I'll be right with ya'," I say. Definitely not for the man who is faint of heart and can go out to any dog park, bar or grocery store and come home with a nubile blonde who doesn't even know what hormone replacement therapy is.

I've just arrived at the point where I really don't spend too much time thinking about OW, but now, after this event, I once again have became obsessed with her. Her long blonde hair, her flawless Swiss skin the color of honey, her almond- shaped blue eyes, her unbroken hairline. Menopause has knocked the wind out of me. According to my calculations, she probably had ten years before she was stricken with crackling vagina and the ten extra pounds that would be with her for life. It hit me square between the eyes. I'm getting older, but OW is just now coming into her own.

When I was married, I really didn't worry too much about menopause. I knew it would come eventually and Mark would be okay when I needed the air turned down during my hot flashes and not be upset that I was cranky sometimes. He would understand. We would get through it just like we got through the pregnancies. Together.

Now I'm going through it alone as he builds a new life with an ovulating woman.

There was only one thing to do after receiving news like this. I put a call out to the Girls' Night Squad. I called Stacy first,

"We have to go out tonight."

"Why?"

"I'm in menopause."

"Oh, boy. Okay, I'll make the calls. Ozona Blues tonight at seven."

Later that evening, I decided to go to the bar a little bit early, just to see if I could attract some male attention, as it was really hard to tell when I approached the bar with my whole posse just who the men were looking at. I liked to assume it was me, but my guess is it was really Stephanie Daniels, with her long streaked hair, thumb ring, high-heeled sandals and the cigarette dangling from her mouth, that really drew their attention.

I hoisted myself up on a stool and perused the surroundings. There were two men across the bar from me, engrossed in conversation and three women a few seats down all wearing loose tank tops and long khaki shorts with belts. Surely, I could beat out three women who had either just come from zoo keeping or hiking the Serengeti.

The bartender came over and asked what I was drinking. I decided to go with my new favorite, the dirty martini. I love ordering this drink. I think it makes me look cool and sophisticated. I like to pretend I'm someone who has clients, unwinding after a long day. I could tell by the way the bartender said, "So, what will you have?" that he was obviously flirting with me, and I would be very surprised if I even had to pay for this drink.

"I'll have a dirty martini, and I like it reeeaaallllllly dirty, if you know what I mean," Wink, wink. "Oh, and two blue cheese-stuffed olives!"

"Come on, really?" he asked, disgusted. "I'm going to have to go back there and stuff some. Surely you can just do pimento stuffed ones tonight? We're really busy out here."

So, this is what it's come to. I can't even get a stuffed olive anymore. I feel like the word *menopausal*, is written in black marker across my forehead.

"Okay," I conceded. Why fight it?

I sat there sipping on my martini and removing the pimentos from my olives with a toothpick, waiting for my "gals" to show up. Finally, I felt a little tap on my shoulder and turned to find Stacy and Stephanie Daniels, who's in full girl's night regalia—leggings, stiletto sandals, diamond toe ring and blazing cigarette—standing behind me,

"I came as soon as I heard," Stephanie said, with a hug and little drop of ash on my shirt.

"Yup, we're here for you," Stacy agreed, ordering her vodka tonic with fresh lime.

Stephanie put in her order for a Corona and planted herself on the barstool next to me.

"So, how did you find out?" she asked, in her deep baritone.

"My doctor told me. Not only that, she suggested I might want to start exercising before my go-to outfit goes from sweat pants and hoodie to an XL muumuu." I took a long swig of martini.

"So? Stephanie said, after sucking on her lime and dropping it down into her beer. "I work out every day. My personal trainer, Jerome, takes me through the whole weight circuit and sometimes I do Zumba. It won't kill you to shake that booty a little bit."

Looking at Stephanie, her twig legs, melon boobs and oversized head I realize she's right. It's time to get serious about my health. Though a personal trainer was not in my budget, surely I could afford maybe the YMCA. I promised myself to go online, check the schedule, and sign up immediately.

"In the meantime, what's going on with your dating scene? Have you seen a penis yet?"

On this note, I brightened up a little bit. I had actually been communicating with a man online that was making that little tingle-tingle in my nether region come back to life, Kramer1. He had reached out to *me* and that alone was exciting. His e-mails were witty and sexy and he was super tall and looked like he had good hair. Also, he looked like he smelled good.

"Actually, no. But, I do have another prospect."

"Great," Stacy chimed in. "How does he look in a Santa hat?"

"Thank you for that," I said as she and Stephanie snorted out alcohol through their noses. "He happens to be a VP for an Internet company and is six foot, six." This got their attention.

"When are you meeting him?" Stacy said.

"Next Friday, actually. He's calling me this week to firm it up."

It was going to be my first date after the doctor debacle, and I was excited about it. Kramer1 had made me promise that I look like my picture because he said, "If you are really that gorgeous, I won't be able to keep my hands off of you. Be fore-warned." He also promised that he made a mean dirty martini and was stocking up on vodka. I took this to mean he planned to have me over at some point. It was a little scary, but I needed this. Bad.

After one more cocktail, the girls and I parted ways and I headed home to get online to join the Y. Possible naked time with Kramer1was great incentive. I envisioned us meeting and having the type of connection where we can't keep our hands off each other. A few weeks later, after endless nights of hot, steamy sex and post-intercourse cuddling, we become boyfriend and girlfriend and he meets my kids who love him, followed by the realistic outcome of a wedding where my sons walk me down the aisle and my daughters are both maids of honor dressed in, hmmm...light pink, I think. So, yeah, I was excited.

I logged on to the Y website and saw I could get a singles membership for just thirty dollars per month. I would have to make the sacrifice. I would find another way to make a small cutback in order to save my body. Once I paid, I was able to log on to the class schedule. I really felt a class would be the best way for me to start, as I would have to be there at a certain time and stay for the duration or call attention to myself by leaving early and have everyone stare at me as I left, all thinking I was a menopausal loser.

I went down the list of classes. Step aerobics was out. I had almost broken my ankle when I tried it ten years ago. I have no rhythm and kept tripping over my step. Body Pump? Push myself to the limit using weights and ropes? That sounds horrible. Then I saw *Cycling: Pedal Your Way to a New You.*

Now that sounded totally doable. Even I could ride a bike, and I am looking for a new me. Perfect. I entered my name and pressed the ENROLL button.

In the morning, I was faced with a huge dilemma. What does one wear to cycling? I decided right then and there that I was not going to turn my workouts into fashion shows. Plus, I doubted I would be running into anybody I knew at the Y. All my friends still had husbands and country club memberships. After digging around in my drawers, I came up with the perfect outfit: My "Mrs. Pitt" T- shirt, a gift from my kids last Christmas, and my red stretch pants that Mark had given me on a Valentine's Day long past. I almost started to put on makeup but decide not to. I'm taking my exercising seriously. No makeup, which unfortunately also means no eyebrows, but whatever, and I did not volumize my hair. It was down and dirty time.

I drove over to the local YMCA feeling energized and excited about my upcoming transformation. I parked and headed in, but was waylaid by a Lulu Lemon gang—five women with blonde ponytails and yoga mats gathered in front of the door. I pushed my way through, not wanting to be late for my first cycling class. " Excuse me," I said quietly, eyes downward.

"Oh, no problem," the big one said as they made a hole for me to walk through. I could feel their eyes staring at my back, and…was that a little giggle? I thought to myself, "Would it have killed you to draw on your eyebrows?"

I signed in at the desk and asked the reception person where the cycling room was. I headed on over, pulled open the door to my new sexy, anti-menopause body, and was greeted by a very bossy lady holding a clipboard.

"Hurry up!" she yelled at me, "Pick a bike. The photographer wants to get started and we're already way behind."

Photographer? What? My gut was telling me leave now. No good will come of this. However, I knew that if I left now, I would never return and would still continue to pay the thirty dollars every month because I'm too lazy to come in and sign the form to deactivate my membership.

I hoisted myself up onto a bike in the middle of the room and glanced over at the pre-teen next to me who was in blue bike shorts and a pink sports bra. Obviously she didn't take her exercise seriously like I do.

"What is going on?" I asked her.

"The paper is doing a story on the benefits of cycling classes," she replied breathless with excitement. "It's going to be on the front page of the *Style* section next Sunday!"

I ask you, is this fair?

Then the photographer came over and asked me and the pre-teen to change places, putting her right in the center of the shot and me off to the side, where I assumed they would be easily able to crop me out. He placed a hand on her shoulder while she got herself situated and told her to run some lip gloss across her naturally plump lips as he messed with her hair.

Before I knew it, *Where Them Girls At* came blasting through speakers that, lo and behold, were right above my bike, and the cycling class began. One hour later, after many encouraging shouts like these…

"Push! We're taking this hill!"

"It's your ride! Make it count!"

I climbed off the bike, my calves throbbing. Other places were throbbing, too, but not in that good way. I was soaked with sweat, but you know what? I kind of liked it. On top of that, I would have the bonus of seeing the left side of my ankle on the front page of the newspaper. Ahh. Life is good.

You will be very proud when I tell you that I went to spin class three more times that week and even invested in a pair of bike shorts and a top with a built in sports bra. It was probably my upcoming date that spurred me on.

I was actually in Walgreen's studying the different brands of teeth whiteners, when Kramer1 called to confirm our date for that Friday night.

"Hello?" I answered tentatively.

"Amy? This is Kramer1, or Ron as I like to call myself."

"Oh, hi. How are you?"

"Great," he answered, "Just confirming our date for Friday night."

"Yes, that should work for me," I answered as if I hadn't been preparing for it since our first e-mail.

"Catch 321 at seven? I'll meet you at the bar. Can't miss me. I'll probably be the tallest one there and will have a red rose in my lapel."

Uh oh. A red rose in the lapel? What's that about? I'm sorry, will you be coming from your brother's wedding? Slight red flag here, but, still, I have to tell you that my heart was beating out of my chest. I felt sexy just talking to this man. Yes, of course the rose in the lapel was over the top, but it was the way he took charge of the phone call and actually made the phone call that mattered. Even his man voice had me all revved up. I felt excited, hopeful, and young. Something fabulous was happening to me.

See, the down side to being married, I think, is there's no way to stay married and get the feeling I got while standing in the dental isle of Walgreens holding a box of whitening strips. I'm divorced so I could be wrong, but I promise you, we tried. We did alone trips; I bought a black nightie now and then, shaved my legs in the summer and tried date nights. Some date nights were great in that we found the perfect place for grilled salmon and a great Pinot Noir. Other date nights were filled with silence and that *I'm missing Project Runway for this?* feeling.

Our last date night happened about a week before my final meeting with Donna Ford, the private investigator, and the incriminating video. We decided to go to my favorite place, Island Way Grille on Clearwater Beach, where I loved to sit by the water as the sun set, slurping down oysters and drinking ice cold chardonnay.

The hostess had seated us at a beautiful table, and the setting was perfect. We took our seats, put our napkins on our laps, and turned to look at the slowly vanishing golden orb. We sat in silence. The waiter brought my chardonnay and I took a sip, looked across the table at Mark, and began to cry. He said nothing. I think even then I knew, deep down, sometimes you just can't go home again, especially when your husband has been playing house with someone else.

Did I hope to remarry? Hell, yes! But I was going to enjoy this feeling, every freaking minute of this feeling. Perhaps I had stumbled onto the upside of divorce. Up until now if you'd asked me to describe myself in one word, it would have been *left*. That is how I saw myself. A woman left by her husband, alone and abandoned. But now I was beginning to feel, if not happy, then at least hopeful. My life was filled with possibilities, and I had begun to realize I most definitely was not alone.

I had been continuing to post my blog, *Ex-Wife New Life*, on a weekly basis. What I thought was a good therapeutic outlet—as opposed to my other outlets: bed, TV, and wine—was turning into much more than that. Women who were going through the same heart-breaking experience had begun to write me and share their stories.

On top of that, I had posted a few blogs on the website *First Wives' Social Network*, and they'd written to ask if they could feature my blog on their home page. I was honored, but more importantly, I felt I needed to be strong for these women who were just starting down a long road I had already traveled. I wanted to be there for them, not in an advising capacity, but in an "I know exactly how you feel, but you're gonna be okay" capacity. With each letter, I could feel the pain and fear they were experiencing, and I wanted them to know that, in time, they would be all right. Me having a pleasant dating experience and sharing it with them, I hoped, would help boost their morale, not to mention my own self-confidence.

The morning of my date, I awoke feeling more energized than I had in a long time. By now, you're familiar with my pre-date regimen, so I won't bore you with that. But I will tell you that I think I looked pretty hot. Skinny jeans, albeit over a pair of SPANX, black T-shirt, and the pièce de résistance, my Steve Madden patent stacked heels, worked together to create the perfect date look. I styled my hair and, luckily, enough had grown back on the short side so my head looked pretty even, with long bangs swept down over one eye. I did my makeup carefully, drew on the perfect brows and finished it off with a brush of pink lip gloss. I felt damn good.

Still, I was extremely nervous as I drove to the restaurant. My gums were tingling from all the whitening I'd done. I have a lot of gum recession, unfortunately, and I certainly hoped it was not all for nothing.

I entered the restaurant, made my way to the bar, and there he was, all six feet, six inches of him, in a black sports coat with the red rose peeking out from his lapel. He was leaning against the bar, looking at me, and I felt like I would melt right there. He was gorgeous with thick, white curly hair and horned rim glasses. As I got closer, I could see that his eyes were a sparkly blue. We gave each other the usual greeting hug, my eyes only up to his nipples. He pulled out a bar stool and I climbed on, our eyes locking.

"Well, I'm certainly not disappointed," he whispered into my ear. "You are gorgeous." He ran his hand up my back, slowly, and then ordered me a dirty martini. "Better make it extra dirty," he told the bartender, who, by the way, didn't protest when he asked him to throw in two blue cheese olives.

We just looked into each other's eyes and smiled. We couldn't stop smiling. I took a demure sip of my drink and waited for the heat to make its way down and unclench my stomach. We started with the usual chitchat about the weather, the traffic, and favorite foods. I'm sure I impressed him with my answer,

"I like cheese," when he asked what I liked to eat. I loved the way he stood, leaning toward me instead of sitting on a barstool. He was so...big.

Over appetizers, we laughed about previous dates. I told him about the doctor and he told me about the woman who showed up with only one leg. Suddenly, as I was reaching for a mini crab cake, he leaned down and kissed me—deeply, you know, with tongue—the whole bit. I closed my eyes partly to let myself totally get swept away into the passion of the moment but also to avoid looking at the rose in his lapel, which seemed to be saying, "Yeah, he's great, tall and sexy, but why am I here? What's that about?"

"Sorry," he said. "I had to do it. To me a bad kiss is like a bad oyster. I just can't get past it. I had to make sure."

"What do you think?" I asked, glad I'd avoided the blue cheese stuffed meatballs.

"Good," he said, "Very good, and very hot."

I had to agree. Finally, it had happened and I no longer had to worry about how or when it would. I had been passionately kissed by a man who was not Mark. It didn't feel weird or awkward. It felt fabulous.

When the night drew to its unavoidable close, he asked me out for the following Saturday. He was going to out of town until then but wanted to take me to a very exclusive restaurant called *Armani's*, which was on top of the Hilton Hotel, and which also happened to be very near his apartment. First off, a Saturday night date is BIG. This means a guy is not embarrassed to be seen with you and is willing to give up trolling the bars on a busy Saturday night to take you out. Secondly, he mentioned it was near his apartment. Why mention that if he didn't want to take me there at some point in the evening? Perhaps for after dinner drinks on his balcony, which he told me overlooked the water. What could be more romantic?

After a very intense good-night kiss, I drove home floating on air. I came down pretty quickly when I found Heather, a strange boy and a pit bull puppy in my den, all three of them glued to an episode of *Intervention*.

"Um Heather?" I politely inquired.

"What?" she answered, eyes not leaving the television screen.

"I see a dog and a strange boy."

"This is Ryan and Doobie."

"Hey," the young man said, waving his hand in the air in greeting.

Two bad things here: The dog's name is Doobie, which cannot be a good sign, and, instead of heading off to my room to relive the entire evening and beat to death every word I said to Ron, I have to sit watching a tearful goodbye as a young mother of six is hauled off to rehab, just so I can make sure there is no pot smoking, sex, or salsa eating taking place on my couch.

Thirty minutes later after finding out the young mother has been sober for two months, I tell the kids it's late and time to shut it down. Heather sees Ryan and Doobie to the door. Finally, I have the chance to ask, "Heather, really?"

"What? He's in my science class. He just moved into the neighborhood. Don't worry. He's cool." What? Am I talking to Heather or Julie from Mod Squad? I took that to mean he was a nice kid, as opposed to he wasn't going to tell the cops about my heroin stash. Back in the day, the question, "You cool?" meant are you going to tell my mom I smoke pot.

Heather and I had a little discussion that ended with some new rules in place:

1. No boys are in the house when I am not home.

2. When boys are over, all doors are to be open.

3. We don't serve dogs water out of my special rock bowl from Sausalito.

Once we had all that established, I was able to head to my room, where I relived every word and each kiss over and over until I finally fell asleep, without, for the first time in years, turning on my DVR.

Chapter 11: How to Fold a Fitted Sheet

"Say goodbye to those crinkly balled up messes."—Martha Stewart

Needless to say, the week leading up to my Saturday night date with Ron was a blur filled with Vietnamese technicians ripping off my body hair and several shots of Botox right between the eyes. Please don't judge. I only visited Dr. C., my plastic surgeon, twice a year now and that was just for the Botox that kept my disappearing eyebrows from meeting in the middle of my nose. Is it vain? Yes. Is it an expense that I don't need? Yes. Did I have a very bad experience when I tried to cut corners and obtain it through other means? YES.

A while back I'd been driving home from Publix and saw a sign at the strip plaza across the street that said, "BOTOX $10.00 per unit." Well, who could pass that up? I stopped in and guess what? You didn't even need an appointment! So I let the doctor/strip plaza landlord, inject my face in the necessary places, which he said also included the frown lines around my mouth. I also realized that a Botox unit is the size of a pinhead and I needed forty-six of them. So much for a great deal.

The following morning, I started off the day with my usual beloved cup of Dunkin Donuts coffee, only to feel my first sip dribble down my chin and land on my pink terrycloth robe. The second sip produced the same result. It became abundantly clear that I had suffered a stroke during the night.

Surely, my legs wouldn't be able to carry me to the hallway bathroom, so I crawled along the floor, inch by painful inch, thinking, why me? I had visions of myself living in a wheelchair with a blanket on my lap, breathing through a straw. Not to mention, this was bound to be a huge turn-off for Ron on Saturday.

I fought to stay lucid and aware as I made my way into the bathroom and pulled myself up to the mirror above the sink. Expecting to see hideous facial distortion and drool, I saw only a series of tiny red dots above my lip and then it hit me—the extra Botox. Phew.

Anyway, by Wednesday afternoon, I was plumped up, nicely coiffed and ready to focus on my dating attire. Once again I went shopping in the cocktail dress section of my closet and this time chose a lovely black Alice and Olivia sleeveless sheath. I would pair that up with some old Jimmy Choo black stilettos. The sky was the limit with a man who was six foot, six. I could wear the tallest shoes in my closet and still feel little and feminine against this guy.

This date was very important to me because it was a second date and because I was very attracted to this man. Very. I knew that in all probability something, you know, sexual was going to happen and the thought thrilled me. What? No. Having sex with someone on the second date does not make me a slut. Not at this age. I deserve to feel sexy, beautiful, and wanted. We all do.

Of course, I realize that part of this intense attraction was that Ron found me desirable and made no bones, excuse the pun, about it. Keep in mind, I was cast aside for a younger woman who probably reeked of green apple shampoo and still carried an emergency tampon around in her purse. I felt used up, cast aside, and old. Ron was offering me new life as a sexy mid-life woman, still very much desired by a man. I was going to bask in it.

Along with preparing myself for the upcoming event, I was still in search of employment. I'd been perusing Craigslist daily looking for the perfect opportunity, preferably one where I could make a ton of money working from home one day a week. The following ad intrigued me:

Holistic Health Spa, looking for concierge front desk per-

son, to make appointments, greet clients and keep up social media. MUST BE HEALTH CONSCIOUS. Apply in person. Eight dollars per hour. Namaste.

Cha-ching! What could be more perfect? Who is more health conscious than I am? Also, it was right around the corner from my house. I decided to pop in that day and offer my many services. I went to my closet to choose the perfect interviewing outfit. What does one wear to work at a holistic spa? Caftans? Flowy pajama pants? Some type of intricately embroidered robe and head wrap?

I chose a bright green Rachel Roy dress and some gladiator sandals. True, they had seen better days and now resembled the sandals Charlton Heston wore in *Ben Hur*, but still, they were passable. I borrowed some peace sign earrings from Heather to complete the look and headed on over.

The spa is literally ten minutes from my house in a little strip plaza right across from the infamous St. Pete Bagel shop. Could this be any better? I park and head inside where I was greeted by a lovely young woman in her early thirties, with long flowing dark hair. She's wearing a long maxi dress and flip-flops. This is a boss? She introduces herself as Maisie and takes me back to her "office," which is a room with soft violet lighting, a small fountain tinkling in the corner, and a massage table made up with crisp white sheets and a dark purple velvet throw.

I've never bought into the whole holistic thing, you know, what with being a huge believer in prescription drugs and all. I did try a meditation class once, which promised to relieve my stress and anxiety. Unfortunately, I found it impossible to sit on a mat and close my eyes surrounded by a group of barefoot people. You know how I feel about feet. I just knew they were pointing at me and laughing behind my back while I sat there cross-legged like an idiot with my eyes closed. I ended up staring at the longest hair I have ever seen, growing out of my right ankle, and left there totally paranoid and more stressed out than when I arrived. However, now it was all I could do to keep myself from climbing onto that welcoming table and let myself be worked on in a holistic way, whatever that entailed.

"So," she began. "Tell me a little about yourself."

Ah, where does one start? I am a divorced mother of four, love long walks on the beach, am comfortable in jeans and formal gowns...oh wait, that's for something else.

Basically, I filled her in on my employment history, which she didn't seem that impressed with, but then she came alive when I told her about my blogging.

"Wow," she exclaimed. "I think my clients will really relate to you. Let me tell you a little bit more about us. I am a naturopath and do lymphatic massage as well as hormone testing and vitamin C facials. We also have two massage therapists on staff, as well as a hypnotherapist. You will be in charge of the front desk, some light housekeeping, as well as keeping the towels and sheets washed, folded and well stocked. Is that okay?"

I nodded enthusiastically as if my lifelong dream of laundering linens was finally coming true.

"I know this is anal," she continued, "but I'm really picky about the sheets. I want the fitted sheets folded nice and crisp and put inside the pillowcase with the flat sheet. Towels must be folded right from the dryer and stacked neatly in rows."

"Oh, don't worry," I assured her. "I'm a mother of four. I have washed and folded tons of sheets."

This was sort of a fib. True, I had washed tons of sheets, but from there they were rolled up into balls and stuffed into overflowing linen closets. Still, come on, how hard could it be?

"Oh, one more thing. Do you live a pretty healthy lifestyle? I mean do you try and eat healthy?"

"Of course," I answered, but the sweat began to bead along my forehead as I glanced outside at my car and saw the straw from my Big Gulp peeking out above the dash. "I mean, I try not to eat a lot of meat.

"Okay, great. Come in Monday at nine and we'll get you started. By the way, we're caffeine and sugar free here. We supply all the herbal tea you can drink, but please don't bring in coffees, lattes, you know, any of that stuff. It will taint us."

Yikes! Well, she didn't say anything about bagels, at least. That could have been a deal-breaker. She handed me a key to the place and told me to let myself in the back way when I came to work. I should note here that the key had tiny flowers on it, and I loved it.

Who would have thought that the prospect of folding laundry for a living at eight dollars per hour could have filled me with such intense pleasure? Years ago, seriously, if someone would have told me this, I would have assured them they had me confused with someone else, or flung myself down on the floor, unable to take another breath from laughing hysterically. I drove home filled with such light, it was as if a cloud had been lifted. I could see a path taking shape ahead, and it was one I wanted to travel. I had a job. I had a date. I had a new life.

Let me clarify this does not mean happily ever after. Of course, I realize a job at eight dollars an hour is not the answer to my prayers. Yes, I also know this date may just be a date, not the beginning of a long-term relationship/marriage culminating with a honeymoon in Napa, after a walk down Rodeo Drive where I look for the Real Housewives of Beverly Hills. It just means I see now there are possibilities, and I felt anticipation instead of fear.

The rest of the week flew by and before I knew it, date night had arrived. The plan was for me to meet Ron at his place and then we would drive to the restaurant together. This was far out of my comfort zone, but something I had to do. I tried to remind myself I was a strong, independent woman and would not do anything I wasn't totally comfortable with. Plus, it was reassuring to know my car was in the parking lot if I needed to make a quick getaway.

The deep British baritone of James, my GPS guy who I imagine looks like Prince Charles with better hair, directed me over the Howard Frankland Bridge into Tampa. Ron's apartment complex was kind of near the airport and the body of water he had mentioned was a scum-covered pond. I made my way up to the second floor and knocked on the door, heart pounding out of my chest.

"Please God," I prayed. "Please do not let him have a rose in his lapel."

He opened the door, and I about melted. He had on brown slacks, a nice long sleeved shirt and brown tie shoes. He smelled amazing. His blue eyes sparkled as he gave me the once over. "You look beautiful," he said, "And oh so sexy." He ran his hand slowly up my arm. "How about a martini before we head over?"

Never one to turn down a martini, I gladly accepted. He led me out to the balcony that did indeed overlook the water/pond and pulled me towards him for a long, hot kiss. I was getting the sense that perhaps *Armani's* may not really be on the agenda, even though I'd already Googled the menu and had my heart set on the Beef Wellington. I pulled away and sat down on one of the little plastic chairs.

"It's really pretty here!" I yelled as a plane heading in for a landing skimmed the top of our heads. "Are those your daughters?" I asked pointing to a photo of two rather heavyset kids on the coffee table.

"Yes, those are my girls, Carmen and Louisa."

"How often do you get to see them?" I asked.

"They live in California with their mom, so I go one weekend a month and we have a blast. They come here for two weeks in the summer. They love this place."

I was sure they did. California can't hold a candle to this little waterfront paradise in the direct flight path of the Tampa International Airport. Still, I figured I would meet them eventually and hoped Heather wouldn't be too mean to them when we got all the kids together.

"Well, I think we better leave or we may not make it over there at all," Ron said, looking at me intensely. Oh, it just sent shivers up my spine and all that. The martini had settled in and its warm glow was just beginning to make its presence known.

"Yes, I think we better," I agreed.

We got into his little blue convertible, and headed to *Armani's*, which is one of the few restaurants in Florida where men are required to wear jackets and the waiters are in tuxes. Luckily, he did not ask to put the top down because I would have had to say, "Oh yes, that would be great," and act like I love the wind blowing through my hair, when in fact I had spent thirty minutes piecing over all the thin spots with hair gel the consistency of super glue. We zipped up to the top of the Hilton where the restaurant had amazing views from every window. The maitre'd greeted Ron by name, and I got the feeling he was a familiar face around here. Sort of like everyone in the place knew something that I didn't.

A pretty young hostess led us to a beautiful table, set with shiny white china and crystal wine glasses and...oh no. There was a rose on my plate, a long red rose. What's with this guy and the roses? What am I supposed to do with it now? Am I supposed to carry it home with me, walking through the restaurant like an idiot carrying a half dead flower?

He picked it up and tapped my nose with it, "For you, because you are so goddamn pretty."

Okay, the whole rose thing was growing on me.

He began by ordering a bottle of my favorite pinot noir, La Crema. We talked over our wine and salads. Several times he reached over and took my hand, once even bringing it to his lips. He was very funny, telling me stories about friends of his, one that involved accidentally breaking into a bank. I tried to find out a little bit more about his work, but he was somewhat vague, saying that he had to travel every week for business but that he loved it. I had Googled his name and the company and found he was indeed a VP there, so that was reassuring.

By the time my Beef Wellington showed up, I was sort of tipsy and very smitten. Dinner was really enjoyable, though I kept wiping my chin, fearing pieces of flaky crust stuck to my lower lip. The waiter came, removed our plates and, I have to say, I was a little deflated when Ron insisted on ordering the Panna Cotta for dessert. Not because I'd rather have the Crème Brulee, but because I wanted to get on with it, already. Come on, let's do this thing!

Finally, the check came and Ron quickly paid, which was a good thing because the wine was catching up with me. If we didn't get back to his place and start making out in the next ten minutes, I was going home to put on my old gym shorts and surf Facebook. He took my elbow as we made our way to the exit, which sort of creeped me out, like I was his old aunt or something, me carrying a dead rose that was leaving a trail of petals as though a bride was about to come through, while the waiters all lined up to say good-bye to Ron. There was something weird about it, and I began to think maybe it was some kind of kidney-stealing trick. You know, Ron lures women in through Game Set Match.com, has dinner with them at *Armani's*, then takes them back to his place where the waiters come over and cut our kidneys out to sell on the Internet? The sad part is I was willing to risk it.

In the car on the way back to his apartment, we didn't talk, though he laid his hand on my thigh, looked over at me and smiled. I did some quiet self-talk: Are you wearing nice underwear? Check. Have you shaved your legs? Check. Then, as a safety measure, I quietly popped a Tic-Tac and a Beano. Game on.

We entered his apartment and fell onto the couch. I have to tell you, I just let myself go. I didn't think about how I looked, or smelled, or my breath, I just enjoyed the fabulous, sensuous pleasure of being with a man. We kissed furiously for a while and then he jostled us around, ending with me lying on top of him. I was losing myself in the kissing, the touching, and the guttural sounds of enjoyment when all of a sudden I felt a sting on my butt. What the fuck? Did I just get bit by one of those giant malaria-carrying mosquitoes that live near stagnant pools of water? Then I felt it again and realized with horrendous shock that Ron was spanking me.

Oh God, what the hell is this now? My first instinct was to jump up and race down to my car as fast as my Jimmy Choos would take me. But then, you know me and peer pressure. Maybe this is what the cool, middle-aged singles do now. I still wanted to be one of the popular kids, plus it didn't really hurt or anything. I just figured I'd been out of the game for quite some time, so, you know, just go with the flow.

Anyway, the night continued on, but I won't fill you in on the details. Let me just say I left a few hours later, drowsy, disheveled and deliriously happy. I arrived home to an empty house—Heather at a friend's and Gabe at his dad's—and took a long hot leisurely bath. I got into bed, relived the night word for word, spank for spank and fell blissfully asleep.

The following morning, I was still basking in the glow while feverishly checking my text messages for anything from Ron. I was expecting "Last night was fantastic, when can I see you again?" or "Get over here, I want you!" or, at the very least, "How was the drive home?" Nothing. Yet.

I did, however, receive a call from Victoria, very interested in how my night had played out.

"So, how was it? Did you get the Wellington?'

"Yeah, it was really good. And I'm totally into Ron, too. I think we really have a strong connection."

"Did you guys do it?"

Somehow my sister, mentally, never made it out of high school.

"I'm not telling you. Gross. Something sort of weird did happen though," I confessed, "He spanked me."

"Oh my God!!! What? Are you serious?"

"Yeah, but it didn't hurt or anything."

"Please tell me you are not planning on seeing him again," she said.

"Of course, I am. We totally are hitting it off. I expect to hear from him any minute. And don't you dare tell Mom, either. That's all she'll think about when I introduce him to her."

Precisely one minute later, my phone rings and I see it's my mother.

"Hi, Mom," I answered.

"Were you naughty?" she said.

In my family, there's nothing sacred. This meant that my aunt in Dallas as well as my sister's friend Laurie in New York, as well as Laurie's therapist, knew that I had received a good old-fashioned spanking, just like a kid getting punished in the sixties, before you were allowed to call Child Protective Services and tell them your mom was making you eat broccoli and request to be removed from your house.

The day continued on without any word from Ron and with

each passing moment, I began feeling sluttier and sluttier. Then I started to make up excuses as to why I'd not heard from him. He probably had to race to California, maybe something horrible had befallen one of his chubby daughters, or the cell service had been knocked out by air traffic control due to his proximity to the landing strips, or even he had dropped his cellphone into the scuzzy pond while going on a run. Yeah, that's it.

In the meantime, I had to prepare for my new job where I was expected to show up the following morning at nine in the morning. I laid out my clothes, maxi dress with gladiator sandals again, and lost myself in a *Chopped* marathon.

I awoke the following morning, surprised to still have not heard from Ron. Heart attack? Car wreck? I felt I deserved a treat after being spanked for no reason at all, as well as seeking fortitude for a long exciting day of sheet folding. I decided I would treat myself to a bagel at St. Pete Bagel Shop, where I had them load up one of their specialties with cream cheese and lox and double wrap it. I got to the spa and let myself into the back with my key, in a real hurry to store my bagel as I didn't want my boss seeing how piggy I can get when it comes to bagels and lox.

I ran to the mini fridge where I opened the door and plunged my bagel into the back, only to send an entire Solo cup of B-12 syringes scattering onto the floor. They all had protective caps on them, so please don't come running to me now if you had a B12 shot over there and got a weird rash or disease or something. I had nothing to do with it. I hurriedly threw them back in the cup and shut the door, my bagel securely hidden behind a molding box of organic strawberries.

The day got off to a fine start. It took me very little time to catch on to the appointment setting system on the computer and printing out the receipts. Unfortunately, the sheet folding did not go as well. Those fitted sheets just would not flatten out and my boss was not happy. "You're really going to have to work on this," she told me. I just nodded and looked around for where I could hide and eat my bagel.

Throughout the day, I checked my phone and each time felt

a kick in the gut when I saw nothing from Ron. At lunch time, I sat behind the dryer and inhaled my lunch, while my boss ran to her holistic chiropractor. The whole Ron thing aside, I felt pretty good about the day so far. The clients were nice, and I talked to one lady who worked for Sam Edelman's shoes. When I showed her my gladiator sandals, she promised to hook me up with some of last year's samples in my size. Sweet perk.

Although I constantly had to pee after, like, twenty cups of pomegranate green tea—without sugar—the day finished out well. Maisie pulled me aside at closing and said, "You did great. Let's just work on that fitted sheet thing. See you tomorrow at noon."

I went home feeling pretty good about my job and really shitty about Ron. When I walked in, I told the kids that after dinner I needed a few hours to research some things for work. They were okay with it as long as they got hamburgers, which they did. Then I headed into my room to obsess over Ron and do my work research.

I went to my computer and Googled *How to Fold a Fitted Sheet* and instantly a YouTube video of Martha Stewart came up showing how to do it. Now let me just say, right here, I love that woman. LOVE. Only MS could start a crochet group in prison and create the "must have ex-con poncho," also known by Lion Brand Yarn as the *Welcome Home Poncho* sought after by yarn freaks all over the world. From all accounts, she was the perfect hostess in prison as well, entertaining cocaine dealers and bribe takers in her cell, and she even taught the gals how to make a perfect plate of nachos. She gave them tips on how to style their hair. They had a going away party for her the night before she busted out and the morning of her departure, an inmate friend practiced her new styling techniques on MS's hair. She walked out of there with her well-coiffed head held high and, from what I hear, a little teary-eyed to be leaving the others behind. Not to mention, if she were a man she wouldn't have been in there in the first place. Just sayin...

Anyway, I took a fitted sheet out of my closet and spent the next two hours following Martha step by step. Sure, my shoulders were sore, but you know what, I can fold a fitted sheet like nobody's business now, which I feel makes me quite marketable.

Once I had that mastered, it was time to focus again on the whole Ron thing. I could not imagine why I had not heard from him. I decided there was only one thing to do, I would text him. I would just put it out there, casually you know, that I had a good time and...and…what? What could I say? How about "Even though you are obviously some kind of sick fuck, I'm dying to see you again?" No, I should probably just thank him for a pleasant evening. I do have manners you know. So I did it. I wrote:

Thanks for a nice evening on Saturday. I enjoyed it. and hit SEND. Then the kids and I watched *Hoarders,* which always makes me feel really good about myself. It was during the removal of the rat skeletons from behind the refrigerator that I received a text from Ron.

I enjoyed it too- out of town for 2 weeks, maybe I will call you when I get back?

Oh boy, that sent me reeling. Maybe? What does that mean? Is he asking permission? He will maybe call me? Why not just confirm our next date? Why can't he call me before he gets back? Is he going to some third world country that has no phone system? Two weeks? That seems like a very long business trip. I was crestfallen so didn't answer back.

The following morning, I cooked a roast beef for the kids, as I wouldn't be home until after seven. I even sliced it up for them. Heather was graduating high school in a few months and was probably quite capable of making plates for her and her brother, but the thought of her wielding a carving knife made me sweat. She has quite the temper. Plus, I still took great satisfaction in providing good meals for my kids.

I also drank two huge cups of coffee since none was permitted into the holistic sanctuary where I was now employed and packed up a plastic baggie of sugar, which I hid in the lining of my purse as if I was carrying cocaine through an airport. Drinking green tea was bad enough, but drinking it without sugar was a punishment I did not deserve. I then headed over to the spa filled with excitement about demonstrating my new sheet folding expertise.

Around five that afternoon, the door to the spa opened and in waddled five of the largest pregnant women I have ever seen. I think I saw a head peeking out from under the skirt of one of them. They were accompanied by their husbands, who were all dressed in Ralph Lauren pullovers, the ones with the huge logos on them. The women were all apparently coming from their jobs as they were all wearing kitten heels and carrying Kate Spade tote bags with a lot of papers in them.

"Hi," one of them said as they made their way in, "We're here for the hypno-birthing class?"

Huh? The hypnotherapist, a very pretty young woman with long blonde hair named Amanda, came out of the back. "What's hypnobirthing class?" I asked her.

"It's a course I offer. I teach pregnant couples how to get through labor by breathing and focusing on something else other than their pain, thereby eliminating the need for any medications."

Okay. It may be just me, but it's very hard to focus on something else when an eight-pound human being is making its way through your vagina with a room full of people staring at your gaping crotch yelling at you to push. Again, maybe it's just me.

Turns out tonight was movie night, where the whole class got to watch a film of an actual medication-free birth, while I served everyone green tea and waters. Before the movie started everyone situated themselves on pillows on the floor, which was a show in itself. Being almost fifty and a towel folder, I was, for all intents and purposes, invisible and was able to listen in on some great conversation:

"Would you believe it? Two people sent us cribs from the Pottery Barn registry. I mean we were dying laughing."

"Yes, we're at Pottery Barn, too, but don't really intend to use a crib, we feel it's actually a way of imprisoning our child."

"Have you looked into preschools? We're already signed up for the two-year-old class at Montessori, but they may be already full."

"We gave the mid-wife a cellphone so we have a direct line

in when we feel that first contraction."

Finally, after I had served everyone their little bottles of water with one mother requesting her water be poured into a glass, and, oh, by the way, do you happen to have a little slice of lemon anywhere?

Amanda dimmed the lights and the movie began. As the woman on the film began her deep breathing, the buzzer on the dryer dinged, so I went back to fold my towels and to sneak a spoon of sugar into my nasty green tea. When I came back out, the woman on the film was beginning her first push. I noticed tears pouring down the face of several of the women. I tried to ignore the whole thing, keeping myself busy by checking my bank account on the office desktop, but then I found I couldn't look away. I was mesmerized by the woman in the film, who was making noises like a water buffalo. I pulled up a pillow for myself and sat down. Before I knew it, tears were flowing down my face and I was totally ashamed of myself for having four epidurals plus demanding pain-killers after each birth. Loser.

When the lights came back on, I passed out tissues to everyone. We all dried our faces, and I collected everyone's trash. Amanda had everyone take part in a group hug, and swept up in the emotion of the moment, I put myself right in the middle telling all the mother's to be, "I know you can do it." They all looked at me, like, "Who are you?"

Anyway, so much for hypno-birthing class. The week flew by and it was in the middle of the next week that I received a text from Ron:

Back at end of week. Friday night?

Don't worry I didn't text him right back. I waited like thirty minutes.

What did you have in mind?"

My place, 7:00 and we will go from there.

See you then.

Yippee! A date on the horizon with a very sexy man. Not just any date, a *third* date, which was even more monumental than a second date. I had a real zip in my linen folding that day. The day had suddenly become much brighter, the towels fluffier, the green tea less bitter.

Friday night, I once again made the trek to Ron's bachelor pad determined not to give in right away to the raging sexual chemistry between us. This time when he opened the door, I didn't allow myself to turn to a quivering blob of desire. He led me inside, we sat down on the couch and he handed me a martini made just the way I like it. I began to make small talk and asked him about his business trip.

Fast forward to three hours later, our clothes strewn around the room and we're lying in his bed, where I was awaiting an invitation for dinner tomorrow night or perhaps the suggestion of curling up together to watch a movie and share a bottle of wine. Ron turned and looked at me.

"Well it was great seeing you again. I know you have a long drive back, so feel free to grab a water from the fridge or whatever."

Um yes, I felt a little whorish. I wrapped myself in a blue throw that was lying on the bed and made my way to the opposite end of the apartment to the guest bath to pee. I absolutely cannot pee, or do anything, with anyone in the room. In fact, I made Mark leave our hotel room whenever the need arose. Not sure if it's a Jewish thing, but my mom told me she didn't poop during her whole honeymoon, which lasted a week, so it's probably inherited.

On my way to the privy, I couldn't help but look into the guest room where I saw about fifty pairs of men shoes lined up against the wall in perfect order. There were huge sneakers and dress shoes. There were ridiculous looking Tevas sandals, and everyone knows I cannot date a man in sandals. Now this is fucking weird. After relieving myself, I went back to the bedroom, put my clothes on, and said goodbye. Ron never got out of bed.

I decided to take him up on the water and opened the fridge. It was loaded with fat free creamer, sodium- free turkey breast and low-cal cream cheese. Oh my God, I think Ron may have been a recovering fatty. Now that I think about it, he did have that little pouch hanging over his groin area that sort of jiggled a little bit. That and the shoe thing took him down a notch in my book.

Things came to a head with Ron about two weeks later. I had received another text about maybe getting together and decided that it was time to figure out where this was going. I told him it would be nice to see him and would he be interested in joining my friend, Bryn Mawr and her boyfriend for dinner the following evening. I felt if he was willing to commit to meeting my friends, than he may be worth dealing with even if he was an ex-fatty with a spanking/shoe fetish. He texted back.

Sounds great. See you tomorrow night.

Well, there was hope. We would begin dating as a normal couple having date nights with other couples and then one day, when it felt right, we would introduce the kids to each other. I just hoped there wouldn't be hard feelings that his kids were chubby and mine were all skinny. Finally, I had gotten this thing on the right track.

The next day, I was one foot into my emergency pedicure when I received the following text from Ron:

Amy really sorry moving to Ohio next weekend and really need to pack. I don't think I can make it tonight.

Of course, I could totally see how that would slip his mind. I told Ming there was no need to polish, erased all his texts, and went home and made my kids spaghetti and meatballs, which we all thoroughly enjoyed.

I will tell you this, it may not have played out the way I envisioned it would, but I had one hell of a ride. Shut up. Also, I still had two kidneys, so there was that.

Chapter 12: Doing Time

"The last place I would ever want to go is prison."—Martha Stewart

It took me a few weeks to recover from the whole Ron thing. At first, I admit, I felt used and slutty and was sort of ashamed of myself. Then I realized, I'm forty-eight years old and have nothing to be ashamed of. I had an enjoyable time with a man I was very attracted to, I learned that men still find me sexy and more importantly, I can still feel sexy. It was my first time out, but I had popped my cherry again, if you know what I mean. I'd also learned it's okay to enjoy a man's company, just for the moment, without planning a rehearsal dinner.

I got right back on the horse, so to speak, and once again tried my luck with Game Set Match.com. Next, there was David. We met at Ocean Prime restaurant, which is quite upscale and swank, and I found him at a side table, making his way through a mediocre bottle of cabernet. After the introductions, he immediately pulled out a photo of his ex-wife, who, he told me, is a hair stylist to local celebs and models, that is, provided they get their hair done at the JC Penney's salon in Westshore Mall. She is an ungrateful bitch and a gold digger. She's moving to California. Who cares? Who needs her anyway? She always takes, never gives. Why is she leaving? Why? How can she do this?

I ordered a martini and inhaled the free bowl of popcorn while David wiped tears from his eyes and poured another glass of wine, after ordering the beef Car Pitch EE o in an extremely loud voice. Around me couples were cozying up by the outdoor fireplace. I didn't want to cozy up to David. I suggested he go to his ex immediately and beg her to stay so that I could finish my drink in peace and order a wedge salad.

Anyway, my membership to Match. Set was coming up for renewal, and I decided to save myself $39.99 and take a break. I needed some time of not logging on to the computer to see if anyone liked me enough to send me a "flirt." Really—and I know it sounds very *Eat Pray and Love*-ish— I needed to take stock of my experiences and figure out what I'd learned so that I could avoid the Rons and Davids on my next go around. I'd just one more date to get through, drinks at a local restaurant called Mystic Fish, with Runningman2000. We'd been exchanging e-mails for a few days when he called me on his way to have dinner with his mother. I found this quite intriguing, both the fact that he called me at the exact time he said he would and, that, on a Saturday evening, he was on his way to have dinner with his mother.

Here's another major difference between dating as a teenager and as a middle-aged divorced woman, I mean, aside from upper body Spanx and very expensive eyebrow pencils. As a teenager, I would never talk to a boy who said he was having dinner with his mom on any given night, much less a Saturday. I probably would have called my friends and said, "Eww, he's such a nerd. He has dinner with this mother!" and they would have all been like, "Eww! Gross!" As a middle-aged woman, there was something that totally turned me on about a man who gives up part of his Saturday to take his mother out to eat. Could it be that he was…nice?

It's true that Runningman2000 didn't have some of the important traits I looked for in a man, which included being at least six feet tall, still in love with his ex-wife and have some sick, perverted tendencies that would come out during intimate contact, which I would choose to ignore and pretend were totally normal. Runningman2000 was only five foot, eight, but he was age appropriate and—tah-dah—Jewish. See above: dinner with mother. I really felt I owed it to my religion to at least try one more before opting out of the whole dating thing.

Growing up, we lived across the street from another Jewish family and the son and I were about the same age. The moms were always trying to get us together, and I fought it tooth and nail, preferring to spend my time with a boy I met who lived in a mobile home park in Pinellas Park and wore his hair like Pony Boy from *The Outsiders*. Mrs. Isaacs sort of took offense that any girl, especially a Jewish one, wouldn't feel honored to go out with her Stevie. She also always told on me when she saw me and Mack McBride making out in the driveway, which would result in me being grounded for a week at a time. Turns out Stevie ended up going to Harvard Law School and last I heard Mack failed out of air-conditioning repair school, so I showed her, didn't I?

Anyway, I knew that if my date with Runningman2000 went the way most of my previous dates did, I could down a dirty martini and be back home within thirty minutes. Mystic Fish was literally five minutes from my house. Still, as the date grew closer, based on my past experiences, I thought about canceling, but for some reason couldn't bring myself to do it. First, of course, was the sheer delight of a bartender putting an ice cold DM down in front of me, but second, when a man tells me he wants to meet me, it makes me feel popular. Yes, I'm ashamed to feel this way, but there it is. I think it stems back to my grade school days when I was always picked last for the dodge ball team. It would be me and Darlene Oglethorpe who had a weird bald spot and a lazy eye, standing alone while the rest of the class was on the other side of the room, already forming bonds with their new teammates. Finally, the cool blonde boy who, at age ten, was in charge of picking the teams as well as sentencing us to years of therapy to repair our destroyed self-esteem, would be, "Oh all right, we'll take Fischler," with a deep sigh. Of course, I now realize these are the boys who played one year of football at the Junior College before dropping out and becoming used car salesmen/financial planners, but it still hurts. Thanks to them, Runningman2000 and I would definitely be having that drink.

I told myself to stop focusing on the downside of dating

and focus on the good stuff in my life. My kids were all doing well. Sure, we'd gotten off to a rocky start, but things had settled down and they seemed happy and adjusted. Mackenzie was living her dream in New York City and so far had avoided further lawsuits with multi-millionaire celebrities. James was living on his own, working for Mark and seemed to be really coming into his own. He was becoming well-respected at the office and it seemed Mark was relying on him more and more. Gabe, my golden child, was doing well in school and had curtailed his nighttime escapades, and Heather was going to graduate high school in a few weeks. I would be on the edge of my seat until I heard her name called at the graduation ceremony, but I'd received no information to suggest that it would not happen. She had no plans for college, at this point, and had taken a job at a local restaurant. She also told me she wanted either a puppy or a baby and I said I'd be happy to take either out for a walk at lunchtime, if she couldn't get away from work.

Yup, they were all doing great, so you know what that means...some shit is about to go down. I was sitting at my desk at the spa, trying to book Mrs. Bennet for her detoxifying footbath, which I hated because guess who fills the footbath and then has to empty it when it's over? I've sloshed dirty footbath water all over myself several times, and I don't know what this nasty brown shit is coming out of these women's feet, but frankly, I don't need it all over my new Free People swing top.

Anyway, while I was trying to talk Mrs. B into a cellulite treatment instead of the vile footbath, I received a text from Heather:

mom police outside. Did you take care of that thing.

That thing? Oh yes, Ha. This is actually a very funny story. See a few months ago, my nineteen-year-old Heather got caught in a local establishment with a fake ID. The funny part is, the young plain-clothed cop who gave her the citation said, "I'm really sorry. This is my first night on the job and my boss is watching. Don't cry. Just go to court and pay the fine and nothing will happen."

Well, you know me and my whole *Midnight Express* fear

of eating maggots in jail. I freaked. I looked at the citation to see when the court date was and there was no date written, nor a case number. I called the courthouse, where a very nice clerk told me there was nothing in their records for a Heather Koko.

I began to think we'd been given a break. Either this guy was so new he didn't know how to fill out a citation, or he took pity on Heather when her big Furby eyes filled with tears and never planned to enter it into the system. I called again a few weeks later and was told the same thing. Therefore, I stuck it in my drawer with the take out menus and Bed Bath & Beyond coupons. That was about six months ago.

I immediately texted back:

they at door?

no just walking around in front of house.

ok let me check on it.

I got Mrs. Bennet set with the footbath, no way out of it, and immediately looked up the number for the courthouse and dialed it with shaky hands.

"Hello, Pinellas County Municipal Court."

"Oh yes, Hello," I said in what I hoped was a nice, polite yet appropriately scared sounding voice.

"My daughter received a citation for a fake ID a few months ago and it had no court date or case number on it. I called several times and was told there was nothing in the system, could you check and see if that has changed?"

"What is the name and birthdate?"

I gave her the information and waited with my heart pounding.

She came back on the line and said, "Yes, it looks like there is a warrant out for her arrest, for failure to appear at her court appearance in October."

Oh fuck, fuck, fuck.

"Well, they kept telling me she was not in the system. What do we need to do?"

"Just bring her down here with the citation and tell them you need a new court date."

"That's it? That's all we have to do?"

"Yes, ma'am. You need to bring her down here."

Okay, well that didn't sound too bad. We would simply go to the courthouse and explain to them this hilarious little story and get a new court date, where we would pay a fine and walk away, free and clear.

I waited until Maisie finished her lymphatic massage and told her I had a slight emergency at home and had to leave. Lucky for me, holistic people are very understanding. I called Heather and told her what we needed to do and to be ready in a few minutes.

"Mom," she cried. "Are you taking me to jail?"

"Heather, no, we just go in, tell them what happened and get a new court date. Don't worry."

I, of course, was scared shitless.

I raced home to get her and saw the police car parked on the street. Turns out someone had broken into our neighbor's garage and Shmaltzy, their Shit-Tzu, was going nuts. The cops were dealing with that issue. Our house was not surrounded with SWAT teams, as we had feared, with snipers on the roof ready to take Heather dead or alive.

We started out and were both pretty quiet on the drive over. When we pulled into the parking lot, I squeezed her hand and said, "Don't worry, we'll get this all straightened out."

We walked into the courthouse and I went right up to the woman sitting behind a huge desk in the middle of the large rotunda. "Hi," I said. "My daughter was supposed to appear in court and we didn't know it because it's not on the ticket, so she missed her court date and we just need to get another court date."

"Wait right here," she said, and then whispered something into a microphone that was clipped to her shirt. Suddenly, we were surrounded by cops. I mean you would have thought I had walked in with Osama Bin Laden and yelled, "Hey guys, look who's here!" Two officers took Heather by the shoulders, and I clutched at her hands. "Back away, ma'am," they said. By now Heather and I were both hysterical and I was yelling, "Don't take her." The woman at the desk was speaking quietly to

Heather, telling her it would be okay, she would have to be taken to the jail and processed and then would be released. Then, and I will remember this to the day I die, they turned Heather around, put her hands behind her back, handcuffed her and led her off to the jail.

I knew I had fucked up.

The woman behind the desk told me where to go, that I would have to post bail and then after she was processed in, she would be released. In the meantime, I called Stacy, who called her lawyer friend, who in turn, gave me the name of a good attorney who deals with this kind of thing. I called him and found out you never walk your kid into a jail. Okay, so now I know. Anyway, he said we would have to go through the process and he would help us from here. We set up a meeting for the following week.

In the meantime, I had to go to the jail building where I would post bail and wait for my little girl. I went through the big glass doors and was stopped immediately at a checkpoint where a big police officer dumped out my purse.

"What is this?" he demanded holding up my plastic bag of sugar that I hid in the liner of my purse.

"Oh, that's just sugar. I work at a holistic spa and my boss doesn't allow sugar, but I can't drink my green tea without it, so I have to carry that."

He stuck his finger in it and then brought it to his mouth. "Oh God," I thought. Who's going to post my bail? I imagined having to call Mark and OW answering the phone and me explaining to her that both Heather and I were in jail and needed him to help us. I pictured her saying, "I'll give him the message," and hanging up on me, leaving Heather and I to become wives to our new cellmates.

Luckily, the officer let me through and I found an ATM where I was able to take out the amount needed for bail, leaving me short on my IRS bill, but I'd deal with that later. I sat there for seven hours until finally, out came Heather. She cried when she saw me.

"I was afraid you wouldn't still be here," she wept.

"Did you think for one minute I would ever leave you?"

A very touching moment ending with Heather saying, "Thanks for taking me to jail. Good one."

I had to hand it to her. She was taking it all in stride. Although a very large woman had come up to her and said, "Gimme yo sammich," when Heather and the other inmates were handed a bologna on white bread, she didn't appear to be too traumatized.

I, on the other hand, was a wreck.

The night before my date with Runningman2000, I found myself alone once again, in the tranquil world of holistic spadom. I had just finished swiffering behind the fountain when, out of the corner of my eye, I noticed the crockpot that holds the hand paraffin was still on. It occurred to me that my hands could use a little TLC and that my cuticles looked like dried up bathroom caulk. Furthermore, I felt that anyone who took their mother to dinner on a Saturday night deserved a date with decent looking hands. So, with Runningman2000 in mind, I took the lid off the crockpot and plunged my right hand into the hot wax. This was not a great idea as I would now have to dial the burn unit with my uncoordinated left hand. Not only was it excruciatingly painful, but I pulled out a hand was that was congealing into a deformed looking claw.

I sat down and waited to see if the pain would die down or if pus filled blisters would begin to form. Eventually, the searing agony did abate and I peeled off the cooled wax, which was actually pretty fun, sort of like picking the glue off your fingertips in Kindergarten. My hand was rather red, but I have to say, quite soft. Yet another sweet perk of the job.

The following evening, I headed off to what I termed my "Last Hurrah." As far as I was concerned, me and my one soft hand would be waving a fond farewell to online dating when I parted ways with Runningman2000, after polishing off my beloved martini. Okay, and maybe the tuna tar tar appetizer, but that was it.

I entered the restaurant, glanced around and spotted him instantly at a high top table in the bar area. He wore a long sleeve black shirt and jeans with what looked like very acceptable loafers. He was reading what I assumed was an e-mail on his phone, so he apparently hadn't seen me come in.

I approached and said, "Ben?" He didn't actually go by Runningman2000. He looked up. "Yes," he said as he stood, smiled and gave me the traditional online date meeting hug. We were the same height. Thank goodness I'd planned for this and wore flat sandals. He was also decidedly cute. Maybe it was his dark brown eyes or maybe his mouth, but there was definitely something.

He pulled the other bar stool out for me and I hoisted myself up on it. When the server came I ordered my DM, extra D, of course, and then something amazing happened. Ben put his phone away. Away. Not on vibrate, lying on the table where he could constantly glance at it as if perhaps something better might come his way, but in his pocket, out of sight.

We made the usual small talk, but even with that, he looked me in the eye and really seemed to care if I thought it was windy today, or if the traffic had gotten worse on Tampa Road. After we were each about half way through with our drinks, he scotch on the rocks, by the way, we loosened up a bit.

"So, do you have any bad dating stories," he asked? "I mean any harrowing experiences?"

And of course I had to tell him about my drunken doctor with the Santa Claus hat and after a few more sips told him how my Anthropologie shawl and I were totally stood up on our very first date.

"How about you?" I said, "Any scary stories?"

"Well, yes. I dated a very nice woman and we were having a great time together. After dinner, we decided to head to a little martini bar down the street. We had a few drinks there and then decided to call it a night. We got into my car and I was having a really hard time backing out of this parking spot. When I turned around to check behind me, she was sitting there topless. It was quite traumatizing." His sly grin dissolved me into laughter, the real kind, not kind the where you're trying to pretend to laugh when you'd rather go home.

And so we ordered dinner.

Throughout the course of the evening, I discovered that Ben had three daughters he adored and seemed to have a very close relationship with. One lived in New York, making her way as a ballet dancer in Brooklyn, and another lived here in Florida and was working in fashion. His youngest was still in high school, in fact, and was just one grade below at my Heather's high school. *Please, I thought to myself, Please don't let it be the girl she almost beat up in the parking lot last week for pulling out in front of her.*

We talked about our marriages and divorces; in fact, we talked about everything. I loved that he only spoke kindly of his ex, had nothing negative to say other than they'd just grown apart. Even now, he still looked out for her, said she would always be family. Just like Mark and I, they had married very young and the marriage had lasted twenty-seven years. He was now living in a typical bachelor condo nearby, so that he could see his youngest daughter frequently, while his ex-wife lived in the marital home.

One thing he told me that I just couldn't fathom was that he and his ex-wife take their daughters out every year for their birthday—together. I had seen Mark only once over the last year and, when I did, I broke into tears. It wasn't anger or regret that caused the tears. I think it was a deep sadness. Although I now knew life would go on and that most likely I would find a new man to share it with, I also knew no man would ever know me the way Mark did. No man would be able to picture me at sixteen walking down a high school hallway. No man would remember holding my hand through the birth of four children. When I looked at James's blue eyes, or saw Gabe's toothy smile, I would always see Mark. While this brought a certain sense of peace, it also brought sadness. I realized divorce is not just the death of a marriage, but the death of a family. I doubted I would ever feel differently.

Ben and I continued to talk until, three hours later, as the bartender began corking the open bottles and the hostess was giving us the stink eye, we made our way to the parking lot.

"I really want to do this again," he said, "And I mean really. What about you?"

"Yes, I think I want to do this again. Sure."

"Just promise me you won't take your shirt off in my car because I don't think I could live through that again."

"Dream on," I said.

He walked me to my car and even unlocked the door for me. I climbed in and he closed the door, after making sure my fingers and toes were in no danger. He was just so damn nice, what my grandmother would call a real *mensch.*

We began to see each other almost daily over the following weeks. The funny thing is I didn't tell anyone. Normally, I'm texting Stacy during a date, telling her what is what: *Oh no, short sleeve plaid shirt!*

However, I hadn't really told her anything about Ben other than I'd found him to be really nice on our first date. People you love have the tendency to pick apart people that you might love down the road. "What? He doesn't like sushi? He's not for you." Or, "Are you kidding me? He uses a Dell? Get out now. He's not for you." I didn't want to hear he's not for me because I was already thinking maybe he was.

Plus, is there anything more exciting than a possible new love interest? There were late night phone calls and silly abbreviated text messages:

CAY –crazy about you

WUB- want you bad

There were stolen hours here and there, if the kids went to dinner with Mark or spent the night out. I went around smiling like an idiot while waiting for the other shoe to drop. There had to be something wrong with him.

I kept looking for his neuroses, weirdness, and OCD tendencies, but, so far, I came up empty-handed. It appeared we were definitely becoming something. Can I call a fifty-three-year-old man my boyfriend or my man-friend? I don't know. But there are several things about him that made me like him more and more. First off, we went for a walk on the beach. Remember, this is Florida, so no one gets to a third date without the required beach walk. During this walk, I learned he played saxophone in the high school marching band. Don't panic. I also found out he runs marathons, likes fast cars and wears cool jeans, so that made up for it.

More importantly, when we returned and were putting our shoes back on, Ben went down on one knee and buckled my sandal. Imagine Cinderella with short brown hair and a size 9 AAA foot. That's who I felt like. He always opened the car door, pulled out my chair and spoke nicely to restaurant servers. He didn't start making those weird grimaces some guys make when the food is taking too long. He waited for me outside restrooms and always let me order my own drink because I told him that was one of the first obstacles I overcame after my divorce.

He was calm, steady and spoke in a quiet voice. He had a great laugh. When he walked ahead of me, he always reached behind him for my hand. We may be the same height, but I felt precious and cared for when we were together. He always answered calls from his daughters and his mother. He was a good person. On top of that, he was fun to be with. It was almost like hanging out with Stacy, but with, you know, a few added benefits.

Heather's graduation day arrived in the midst of my whirlwind romance. For a moment, I thought of inviting Ben, but decided that even though he was becoming more and more important to me, I wasn't ready to bring him into the inner sanctum of my life, which included four children in various degrees of healing and one large dog who was basically a walking anal infection. I really wasn't trying to hide anything, just trying to make sure he was properly prepared.

I'm not sure what was holding me back. Ben wanted to meet them, and I'd already met all three of his lovely, polite, funny and normal daughters. If my kids met him and didn't like him, would I be forced to give him up? On the other hand, what if *he* didn't like *them*? I mean, how dare he? Is he crazy? What's not to like? Sure, we've had some dealing with police, lawyers and the occasional guidance counselor, but come on! They are totally perfect. I'm not sure who I was trying to protect here, but the meeting was being delayed.

I attended Heather's graduation with my parents and Gabe. I knew that somewhere in the huge auditorium Mark and OW were sitting together getting ready to watch our daughter graduate high school. He had asked me if it would be okay for he and OW to take Heather out for dinner afterwards, and I had conceded. Far be it from me to get between Heather and a delicious dinner at Charley's Steak House. I told her to have the lamb chops; they're the best I've ever had. She looked at me as if I had told her to order human remains. Turns out she had just gone vegetarian. Good thing Charley's does a great chopped salad.

Needless to say, I was on the edge of my seat, literally, hoping to see Mark and OW and dreading it at the same time. I'd never actually seen them together, and I wasn't sure how I'd react. Eventually, I spotted them several sections over. They were both looking at the program and pointing at something I assumed was Heather's name. They looked like a normal couple. In fact, they looked like a really good-looking couple, with really great hair in various shades of blonde. They were so…yellow. I watched them for a moment, and then realized, "Okay, this is not so bad. I can do this," Then turned my attention to the stage and waited for Heather to walk across it and get her diploma, which she did, as my parents and I breathed a collective sigh of relief.

After the ceremony, we met Heather in the lobby and took a few pics before she left to meet her dad and be whisked away for a night of celebrating. My parents dropped Gabe and I off at home. We didn't stop for dinner. For one thing, it was only 4:30, and for another thing, one of my father's major goals in life is to beat traffic. It doesn't matter where he's going, or why, but it's extremely important that he make good time. With 5:00 looming and the ride from Tampa to Palm Harbor hanging over his head, we basically ran to our car and drove to my house, where he came to a rolling stop so that Gabe and I could get out.

All was quiet inside. Gabe grabbed his skateboard and disappeared out front, while I went into my room to change out of my graduation dress/bar mitzvah/funeral attire. I also needed to gather my thoughts. I realized in just two more years, Gabe would be graduating and would definitely be off to college. He was my golden child and had no choice. I would be childless for the first time in almost twenty-five years. I was surprised to feel not sadness but a tiny bit of anticipation. In the last two years, I had gone from wife to ex-wife and lived to tell about it. Yes, I went into divorce kicking and screaming and drunk texting with some slight stalking thrown in. But on a positive note, I came out stronger and with some great new underwear. I was sort of excited to see what happened next.

Chapter 13 Sister Wives

"Your basic extended family today includes your ex-husband or wife, your ex's new mate, possibly your mate's ex and any new mate that your new mate's ex has acquired."—Delia Ephron

Several months later, on a fall Wednesday afternoon, the day restaurant coupon flyers come out and I had my heart set on that Pizza Hut pizza with the cheese-filled crust at a two for one price, I walked out to my mailbox, already salivating. I reached in and pulled out not only the Pizza Hut coupons—free drink with purchase, too— but also what appeared to be a wedding invitation in a big, square, gold envelope.

My first thought was, oh my God, I bet it's Kris and Jim Gillum doing one of those idiotic vow renewal ceremonies, where I would be forced to stand on a beach holding a glass of warm chardonnay, my hair frizzing, listening to them recite embarrassing vows to each other, such as:

You are my rock, my light, my very breath.

You are the only woman I have ever loved and will ever love.

I will be your wife all over again—.

Yeah, but on this second go around, Jim, could you please not stare at all Kris's friends boobs, as it really creeps us out? Crap, do we have to bring gifts to these things? They already have a house full of those eerie Hummel figurines.

Then I thought how it's not fair that all the ceremonies that revolve around drinking and getting gifts are related to marriage.

Wouldn't it be awesome to have a Divorce Vows Renewal Ceremony, like you know, I wouldn't divorce you all over again. I mean we divorcees deserve a little celebrating while sharing our heartfelt thoughts, too! I began to tear up thinking of the things I wanted to say to Mark:

I vow to stop opening the wine basket that still comes to you every Christmas from the insurance company, but, in my defense, who can resist a good bottle of Liebfraumilch and a pound of peanut brittle?

I vow to stop calling your old bike shorts my fat pants.

I vow to quit telling the weird pool guy that you still live here.

I could start a real trend here.

I turned over the invitation for further investigation and saw it was addressed to Heather and Gabe. Surely none of Heather's friends were getting married yet? They were still teenagers. Did she have an Amish friend that I didn't know about? Upon closer inspection, I saw that none of Heather's friends were getting married yet. Her father was. My husband was getting married. I assumed James and Mackenzie had received their invitations as well.

I had the feeling of water rushing over my face as I pictured Mark on our wedding day, hair in a military buzz-cut standing there in his rented tux. Almost thirty years had passed since that day. I remember at our reception a waiter asking, "Does your husband want white or red wine?" and me thinking, "My husband." How can you possibly know at age twenty what that word will entail? It doesn't just mean the person I will have sex with for the rest of my life. It means, ups, downs, births of children, deaths of parents, family dogs, family cars, family traditions. Did he really mean to have that with someone else?

I stood there so long that eventually my neighbor yelled, "Hey what's wrong? Is your cat gone again? You guys need to train that thing."

Why was I shocked? I mean, what did I think was going to happen? OW is a young woman. She could even still have children if she wanted. Imagine children out there in the world—

children that I had no connection to— but were sharing a gene pool with my children. I pictured their kids looking just like my kids but with yellow hair and a German/Swedish accent. I gotta tell you this was tough.

Up until now, I was the wife, albeit an ex-wife, and she was just the girlfriend. Now we would be equals. We would share the same last name. Oh my God, two Mrs. Koko's! This blew my mind. It reminded me of last year when I went into the tennis club to rent court time. I had read an article about how hitting tennis balls really hard could relieve stress and thought I'd try it. I gave the lady at the desk my membership number and she typed it into the computer, then looked at me and said, "I'm sorry that number belongs to someone named OW."

"No!" I yelled. "She's the girlfriend. I'm the wife." What would I say now, "She's the second wife?" Most likely I'd have to give up tennis anyway, because I think my kneecaps are turning to chalk dust.

I think the real kicker was I'd always assumed that I'd be the first to remarry. I had assumed, since Mark left the marriage, he didn't want to be a husband. Now it appeared he just didn't want to be my husband.

Later that afternoon, Heather came by to do her laundry. She was now living on her own, which basically meant she slept somewhere else, but took all her meals at our house. She also brought her new boxer puppy, Cassius Clay, with her, who insisted on leaving little puddles of pee next to the pool.

She, Gabe and I were in the kitchen where I was pretending to casually go through the mail.

"Hey," I said. "It looks like you guys got a wedding invitation."

"Yeah, Dad's getting married and we all have to be in the wedding, which sucks," Gabe said as he grabbed a soda and headed to his room.

"When is it?" I casually asked.

"In May. Me and Mackenzie have to be bridesmaids," said Heather, grabbing an cookie from the pantry. "It's so stupid."

I could see the kids weren't surprised by this turn of events, so I decided not to ask why they hadn't mentioned it before now. This wasn't going to be easy for them either, watching their father marry someone who was not their mother. It was hard enough for me to imagine my children being part of a ceremony binding their father to another woman. It would be much harder for them if they thought I was upset about it.

And then I realized I'm well on my way to being okay. Mark and I grew up together and shared a life for many years. He made me a mother, and I made him a father. I loved him and because I loved him, I wanted him to be happy. Could it possibly be that I was coming to terms with my divorce? I thought back and now realized I'd noticed changes in myself, so it all began to add up. First off, the weight I'd lost during my divorce was starting to show back up in weird places like my upper back and under my chin. When I complained of this to my mother she said, "Oh, please. It's nice to have a little shape to you." This is why it pays to have a Jewish mother, even though you'll never outgrow the habit of bringing a sweater to every restaurant you ever eat in "just in case you get chilly."

Of course, the weight gain might be due to the fact I liked food again. It tasted good. I didn't have that horrible stomach churning and burning like I did in the early stages of divorce, when it felt like I was trying to swallow cotton balls. In fact, I may even look forward to my food too much now. Like I wake up and wonder whether I finished that rye bread yesterday, and if I didn't and there is some left, shouldn't I have it with melted cheese because breakfast is a very important meal and I need protein? When breakfast is over, I'm thinking about lunch. When lunch is over, I think about dinner. After that, I wonder what to munch on during my shows, which usually end with my eating two Skinny Cow ice creams, but that's okay because they're Skinny Cows, right? Yes, I know, this could be troublesome.

Secondly, I was now able to get through an episode of *Say Yes to the Dress* without crying.

Lastly, I hardly ever said "motherfucker" anymore, or used it in the subject line of an e-mail. Based on these findings, it was clear that I had almost recovered from my divorce.

Now, let me be clear that this didn't mean I'd be stalking their wedding registry page, trying to find out who was on the invite list. It only meant I'd be doing it to see what kind of China they chose as opposed to leaving obscene messages. It seemed important for me to know if the second Mrs. Koko's decor would be modern or lean towards the conservative. I was sure that she was one of those women with hand-painted faux finishes on her walls. I knew she probably mixed Pottery Barn staples with whimsical furniture she made herself during her free time. I could just see her, her blonde hair tied up in a scarf, with a dot of yellow paint perched cutely on her nose. She would have those big over-sized couches with bright pillows on them and quirky pieces of art on the wall. My idea of decorating was to paint everything white and put a plant in the corner.

She probably liked to have stuff, little end tables and lamps, and those carved wooden signs over the door that say things like "Family Comes First" and "Home is Where the Heart Is." I hate that shit.

Right then and there, I decided it was time to focus on the good stuff in my life. I really liked my spa job. In fact, on top of mastering folding the fitted sheet, I had started a divorce support group with a few of the clients, which was about one out of every three women. Some of them were like deer in the headlights, still reeling from the whole experience, and I hoped we would be able to help each other heal a little bit. It wasn't like, "Hey you guys, just follow my advice and then you too may be able to fold fitted sheets at a health spa." It was more like, "I feel your pain. I get it. There has been a major change of plans and we have to roll with it."

I knew just sharing experiences with others makes us feel less alone. Once a week, we would meet at Starbucks and discuss where we were in the process and how we were feeling. At our first meeting, we were pretty quiet, sitting around sipping our Vente soys and waiting for someone to break the ice. Finally, I began by telling them I spent the first six months of the divorce process wearing a blue Snugly and flip flops, sometimes with a belt, if company came over. Then I told them about my triumphant return to college and how that became a turning point for me. Since I love talking about myself, this was working out really great, sort of like an Amy Koko HBO Special, which is a dream come true, at least for me. Then I suggested we go around the table and talk about what we were feeling, because I was starting to get a little hoarse.

Kelly, who at thirty-two was the youngest in the group with straight blonde hair and a little rosebud mouth, began. She had spent the last year taking care of her elderly mother-in-law who was recovering from hip replacement surgery, in the guest room of the home she shared with her husband, Mark. This included overseeing unspeakable things involving bodily functions, as well as cooking and feedings. Once mom was able to return to her own home, Mark calmly announced he really didn't feel like being married anymore and moved out that day. He was currently living with "She's just a friend."

Kelly was transitioning from the painful disbelief phase to the anger phase and had a long road ahead, but she would make it. This story almost brought the ladies to their feet. They were furious. Another round of Ventes and some lemon bars were ordered as the feelings began to flow.

Esther, sixty-one, told us she'd been divorced for five years. One day she came home from her scrapbooking club and her husband was gone. Gone as in, took his Orvis fly rod from the garage and moved to Montana. She received alimony and had been given the house in the divorce, so she was financially okay but was getting lonely. That, of course, led to the subject of dating. I'm not sure if it was the sugar high or what, but all of a sudden Esther blurted out, "I met a man on *Plenty of Fish!*"

We were all thrilled by this announcement, until we learned the man lived in Canada and was desperately trying to make his way to the US so that he and Esther could meet. So far Esther had contributed five hundred dollars to the cause. We were like, "Esther! No!" We tried to tell her there are men within a ten mile radius that could afford a tank of gas to come meet her for coffee. It was decided, at our next meeting, we would bring computers and work on our online dating profiles.

Another positive was that my blog was continuing to flourish. It was now being followed by people in England, Russia, Albania and even Iran. Goes to show, divorce sucks everywhere. I was thrilled by each comment and took time to answer each one. I was now trying to find a way onto the *Huffington Post.* I spent a good part of my day formulating letters to the editor of the *Huffington Post* divorce section, asking if I could send them a test post. That would be a dream come true, having my blog read by Ariana Huffington, and then she and I would talk about world politics and what an ass Kanye West was. Big dreams. Big.

Also, I was now doing freelance writing and getting paid for it. I wrote blog posts for *Allvoices.com,* where I was able to use my training and expertise to offer insightful reviews of the *Real Housewives* of every city. Countess De Lasepps is still my favorite. I also wrote about Martha Stewart and Gwyneth Paltrow and got paid for it, too. I then took on a "gig" writing for *Therichest.com.* I covered things like the most expensive caviar, the most expensive private islands, and the most expensive yoga pants. Between all of these little jobs, I was actually doing pretty well, which, when you put it in perspective meant that I could now afford HBO.

Another really good thing was Ben. We'd been together over four months now, and I had learned a lot about him. For example, he makes his bed every day. I find this to be unnecessary energy expended, but I can live with it. He doesn't like clutter, which I totally get. I don't consider the year supply of *People* magazines and empty water bottles next to my bed clutter, so difference of opinion there. He believes if something is worth doing, it is worth doing right. I believe if something is worth doing, I'll do it until I get bored and then go look for new emoticons on my cellphone. Still we totally connected on the big things. We both hate store bought bagels, way too doughy, or *goysihe* as Ben said. I get so turned on when he used Yiddish words. Also, we both love anchovies on our pizza, which right there is enough on which to base a relationship. Finally, we both loved a ton of sauerkraut on hotdogs. Beyond that, I felt all other problems could be overcome.

We were now pretty much an item. We're seeing each other exclusively, and though I'd not introduced him to my children, I'd told my kids about him. Mackenzie and Heather seemed happy for me and expressed an interest in meeting him. I said it would happen eventually and explained to Heather that she couldn't call him "dude" or say "fuck," at least not until we knew him better. My boys had a slightly different reaction. When I told James, he said, "Okay, but he better not be a dick." And Gabe's reply was, "Whatever."

I don't think they were thrilled but were probably relieved that now maybe it wouldn't fall on them to help me if I ever fell getting out of the tub. It'd happened to me last week. I'd slipped stepping out of our tub, which, for some reason, had two marble steps that basically turned into wet glass when I stepped out. I fell flat on my ass and thought, "This is how people break hips." After gathering myself, I marched right out to the family room where Gabe and James, who had come by for a plate of brisket, were watching *Storage Wars* and announced,

"Mother has just fallen stepping out of the tub. If it happens again, I may need you to help me."

At which point, they both ran gagging from the room. If nothing else, Ben could save them from that horrible fate.

A few days after the wedding invitation arrived, Ben and I were having dinner at our favorite place, Palm Pavilion. The oysters were fabulous and the view was amazing. Between the sound waves lapping against docked boats alongside the restaurant and the first few sips of my cold DM, I was feeling beyond relaxed.

Ben took my hand from across the table and said, "So tell me, how do you really feel about Mark getting married?"

"I don't know. I feel like I'm okay with it. I was just really surprised."

"Why are you surprised?" He turned my palm up and kissed it and then looked me deep in the eyes. "People who are in love tend to get married," he said. "You know I love you, right? I mean I do. I love you. Maybe we'll end up getting married someday as well."

I did know it. And I knew I loved him, too. He brought me laughter, happiness and something that I had lacked until now: a sense of stability and calm. He was all I could want in a partner and now he was telling me that marriage was in our future.

I waited for the sheer happiness and relief to wash over me. I could be a wife again. Nothing yet. I waited a few more seconds thinking, Has my martini left me numb? And then I realized it wasn't the martini. It was me. I was shocked to discover though I wanted to be with Ben, even be companions for life, I didn't want to be married. I realized with a start that I liked just being me.

This was strange coming from someone who had defined herself by the word "Mrs." Yes, I wanted a companion, a partner, a lover, a best friend, but maybe not a husband. It had nothing to do with Ben. It had everything in the world to do with me. I'd gained a certain sense of independence, a little bit of freedom I hadn't known before. I was afraid being married would turn me back into that woman who values granite and stainless steel appliances above a sense of self-confidence in her abilities. I was anxious to see what our relationship would look like down the road. I wanted us to have the perfect marriage, just without being married. When I told him this, he said, "I'm committed to you. I don't need to give you a ring to make it real."

"But maybe a necklace or something," I replied.

Then he said, "It's really time for me to meet the kids. I know you're scared. They've been through so much. But I promise, I won't make demands of them or expect anything from them. I will prove to them that I love their mother, and, in time, I know they will be happy we have each other. It's like you have that door shut so tight and you're afraid to open it."

I realized he was right. The time had come, and I really couldn't put it off any longer without raising some weird suspicion on his part.

"Okay," I said. "Mackenzie will be in town next week. How about if I plan a barbeque, you know, just something casual and we'll see how it goes?"

"Perfect," he said.

Then, of course, fate stepped in or, as my Aunt Kitty used to say, "We make plans and God laughs." We were on our way home, when Ben's cellphone rang and immediately went to the car's Bluetooth, meaning I was privy to the following conversation between him and his youngest daughter:

"Hi, Daddy!" Such a sweet lilting voice!

"Hi, Honey! How are you?"

"Fine, Dad. Just hadn't talked to you in a few days so wanted to check in."

"Oh, that's nice, honey. How was your weekend?"

"Nice. Went to the beach yesterday and today just doing homework."

Right about that time my cellphone rang. I looked down and saw it was Gabe, probably checking on me, making sure I was on my way home. That kid sure loves his mom. I held the phone up so that Ben could see that my son too likes to check in.

"Hi, Gabe! How's my big boy doing?"

"Fine, Mom. Hold on. This cop wants to talk to you."

I turned to Ben, "Um, could you hang up? I think Gabe's being arrested."

"I have to go, honey," Ben said.

"Hello, ma'am," a deep voice said from the other end of my cellphone.

"Yes," I said. "I'm his mother."

"This is Sergeant Sanders of the St. Petersburg Sherriff's Office. We have your son Gabe here. He's fine, but, you know things get crazy at these outdoor concerts. He was just standing in a place he shouldn't have been. He's not in trouble, but we do need you to come to the concert venue and pick him up."

I'd given Gabe permission to attend the Lil' Wayne concert because it was outdoors and during the afternoon. I mean what could happen? And when would I learn to stop asking that when it came to my kids?

I told Ben the address and, as we made our way to the destination, he held my hand and reassured me. "All kids go through this, really. It's not a big deal. As long as he's okay, and he is. We'll just go get him and everything will be fine. I'm actually excited," he said. 'I get to meet Gabe."

We pulled up to the venue and there was Gabe standing on the corner speaking with two police officers. I ran up to them.

"Hi. I'm Mrs. Koko and that's my son."

"Okay, he's free to go. He's such a great kid."

"Thank you," I said and snatched his hand as we headed towards Ben's car.

"Bye, Gabe," the cops yelled. "Thanks for being so polite!"

Gabe climbed in the back seat and Ben turned around and said, "Hi, Gabe. I'm Ben. You okay?"

"Yeah, I'm okay. Thanks for coming to pick me up, Ben."

Turns out that Gabe was standing in a crowd of people who were enjoying some illegal substances during the concert and was also among the group who were escorted out. Apparently, kindly Officer Sanders believed him when he told them he wasn't part of their group, thus a phone call and a get out of jail free card.

"Well, let's get you something to eat and head on home. What do you feel like?" Ben asked.

"McDonald's, I guess," Gabe said, and a bond was formed between Ben and Gabe over chocolate shakes and large fries.

That night I fell more in love with Ben. Never once did he judge me or tell me how to be a better mother. He offered only support, kind words, and a bag of McDonald's. He dropped Gabe and me off and didn't ask to come in, knowing we probably needed some time to decompress. As he drove away, I was sorry to see him go. I was ready to bring him on to full-time status.

The following evening, I sat down at my computer to kick around some ideas for a blog post and heard my e-mail ding. I assumed it would be the usual e-mail introducing yet another product to enlarge my penis, even though I'd written to this spam company several times to tell them I don't have a penis to enlarge and so please unsubscribe me. My heart skipped a beat when I saw name@huffingtonpost in the FROM line and read:

Your story sounds intriguing, and I'd love to hear more. Are you interested in blogging for HuffPost Divorce? As a general guideline, prefer tightly focused pieces of 500-1000 words. I'd love to hear more about your divorce. Are you open to writing about it?

We all have them, moments in our personal history that change our lives. I had childbirth, the invention of reality TV and now this. For me, this was a game-changer. Turns out my story was not sad, pathetic, and old as time. It was, according to someone who had her finger on the pulse of modern society, intriguing. Am I open to writing about it? Let me get my Thesaurus. How many different ways are there of saying, "Hell yes"?

For the next week, I spent every free moment in front of my computer, trying to write a blog post that was funny, yet meaningful, or maybe something that would have helped me if I'd read it back at the beginning of my divorce journey. I wanted women who had experienced what I had, to know that eventually they'd be able to enjoy food again, they'd have sex again and they'd be able to laugh again. Mostly though, I wanted them to know they would survive. When I hit the *Enter New Blog Post* button on my very own special *Huffington Post* login site, I knew I'd arrived. I was a Real Writer.

A few days later, I received an e-mail that my post had been published with a link to it's location in cyberspace. Here's an excerpt:

MY HUSBAND LEFT ME FOR A SWISS PASTRY CHEF FOR DUMMIES

Here's is what not to do when your husband sits you down after twenty-seven years of marriage and tells you that he has found someone else -- a thirty-year-old, blonde Swiss pastry chef no less. Um... let's face it, there is no competing with that.

1. Do not wrap yourself in a blue Snugly and take to your bed with a box of Captain Crunch, watching infinite hours of "Two and a Half Men." This serves no good purpose and those smashed Crunch Berries are itchy and apparently attract bed bugs.

2. Do not set his Ferragamo shoes and Rolexes on the front lawn with a sign that says "FREE!" It is very embarrassing to have to go collect all these items from your neighbors when you get the cease and desist order from his attorney.

3. Under no circumstances drink a bottle of cabernet at your married friend's house, back up into her tree, and then drunk text your ex ending every sentence with "mother fucker."

Here is what I recommend for dealing with the departure of a husband:

1. Get an attorney ASAP, but do your research. I picked my first attorney because she had the same name as the head cheerleader in high school that I idolized. One year and twenty-five thousand dollars later, I was no closer to being divorced than I was the first day I retained her. However, she did treat me to an endless pasta bowl at the Olive Garden once. Moral of the story, get referrals, get advice and talk to each potential attorney. Read up on the divorce laws of your state. Know your rights and protect yourself!

2. Seek out support. Your married friends love you and feel your pain, but hello—they're still married! Look for divorce support groups in your area, but beware of what I call the "Sad Sacks Divorcees." I went to one meet-up where everyone sat around at a table in a sports bar crying and reliving their stories. This will be enough to put you back in your Snugly with a fresh box of Crunch Berries. If it's not a good fit, move on! I also did a few online groups, including a first wives social network. There you can vent, cry, act out, and read informative articles and no one can see your face.

3. Most importantly, take care of you. One thing I realized once I found myself alone is that I didn't even know me anymore. What were my dreams, desires, new goals? Take the time to figure it out. Believe me, I know how hard it is. I was married for twenty-seven years to a man I met in eleventh grade. I regret a lot of the things I did during our break-up, including horrible text messaging and acting out in front of my children. Above all, try and retain your dignity. This will pass and you will survive, whether you believe it now or not. Be able to continue onto a new life with your head held high. I can tell you from experi-

ence, a new world awaits you, and in time you will embrace it.

I hate to say this, but when I saw this post with my picture above it, you know the one of me on that good hair day that I also used for Game Set Match.com, I felt the same way I did when the doctor laid my babies on my stomach right after they had emerged from my body. It was sort of like, "Wow. Look what I made." I stared at it for what seemed like forever, reread it like seventeen times, thought of a million ways I could have written it better and then sent it to my mother. And my Facebook friends. And my dental hygienist. I was in awe of myself. Then I saw I had one hundred and fifty-nine comments. I couldn't wait to read all my accolades. The first comment read:

Lying in bed eating cereal? No wonder he left you. Get a life.

Okay, that was so not nice. My first reaction was to explain myself, make sure the person who commented knew I only ate Crunch Berries in bed while I was going through divorce and now I take most of my meals at the table. Then I read a few comments where women were thanking me for my post. I felt better and figured not only was my writing going to be read by women everywhere who I hoped would find something of value in the words, but there was the very distinct possibility that Meryl Streep would be checking out the Huff Post blog at her computer in the morning, while eating a piece of rye toast and drinking a cappuccino made for her by her house boy. She would read my post and think, "Oh, yay! I think I found my new best friend," and fly me out to her home in Connecticut, where we would have a great lunch and she would tell me stories about Robert Redford and *Out of Africa.*

Obviously from there, we will talk about my book and how she wants to star in the movie. It's going to be so awesome! Things are really coming together for me now. I'll write a book and Meryl will star in the movie. I mean, that's my plan...

Amy Koko

is a contributor to Huffington Post Divorce, Over 50 and Women sections. She has written for First Wives Social Network and Creative Loafing, a local publication. She has been an active blogger, exwifenewlife.com , since 2011

You can follow her on Twitter at https://twitter.com/female50freaked or friend her on Facebook at https://www.facebook.com/amy.f.koko, where she will always follow or friend you back.

Made in the USA
San Bernardino, CA
02 March 2016